THE GOOD, THE BAD AND THE HOLY

Stories and Musings From A Lifetime of Ministry

BY

Ron Baesler

DEDICATION

Christian ministry is ministry done in community. It has been my great privilege to share ministry with many wonderful communities of faith. This project is a product of my work in their midst. I dedicate this book to the colleagues and families at Peace Lutheran in Fargo, North Dakota, to the colleagues and families in three parishes in the Brazilian state of Rio Grande do Sul:

the Lutheran Parish in Morro Redondo,
the Lutheran Parish in Esteio-Sapucaia,
and the Lutheran Parish in Guaíba;
to the students and colleagues at the Seminário Evangélico de Puerto
Rico, San Juan, Puerto Rico;
and finally, to colleagues and families at Messiah Lutheran in Yorba
Linda, California.

GRATITUDE

My family has been my anchor throughout my ministry. In all of our journeys and ministry challenges they have surrounded me with their love and support. My children, and now their spouses and my grandchildren, have been constant sources of joy. Lin, my dearest friend and wife, my constant ministry partner, has endured our many ministry moves with grace and creativity, and continues to amaze me with her energy and enthusiasm for life. Without her, this book would not be, and I would not be me.

CONTENTS

THE GOOD, THE BAD AND THE HOLY
Stories and Musings from a Lifetime of Ministry

1. MY FLESH, MY SPIRIT, MY WORD
(An introduction)

"Them's fightin' words, mister!"

"I give you my word."

"And the Word became flesh and dwelt among us."

Word. Is there any thing more human and less substantial than a word? How can something so ambiguous and amorphous as a word inflame passions, ignite wars, or melt hearts?

What are words after all? Ethereal vibrations of molecules set in motion by air propelled past fleshly cords in my throat, rippling across the space between us, striking the tiny timpani in your ear, stirring miniscule bones in your skull whose tremors stimulate nerves that transmit neuronic signals to your brain.

What are words after all? Tiny marks—lines, curves and squiggles—have been laid across a screen or page. Light waves reflect off of them and ripple through space. These energy pulses strike the cells in my eye, trigger an electrical reaction which races through the optic nerve to my brain and suddenly somewhere in that mysterious world called "mind", an idea is born, an object is imagined, or an emotion is generated.

Words. Are they mere symbols? Do these invisible vibrations in the air, these resonances of light simply stand in for that which is real? Or, are words part of the warp and woof of reality itself? A thing without a description, a thing without a name—is it not in some sense less real? If I have an experience of any sort but have no words whatsoever to talk about it, even to myself, how real an experience is it? Words help to create, or at the very least, help to complete what we humans call "reality".

Words are my passion. I was an early talker. Talk, talk, talk. More than once as a child I would get so enthusiastic about sharing a bit of news that my vocal system would overload and shut down. As Mom explained it, I had so many words inside of me, they'd create a logjam in my throat, and I'd stand in front of her sputtering and stuttering. Very early in life I learned how to avoid logjams. And thankfully, I do not always need to talk when I am around other people. I deeply treasure silence.

But I am still passionate about the spoken and written word. Telling a good story gives me goose bumps. I savor the skill required to tell a joke. I yearn for the chance to preach. I crave the opportunity to teach. Weaving my words together with another's words in a forum or a discussion—what a rare privilege. I cherish the ability to speak words that inspire, inform, challenge, console and guide. Speaking in front of people and sensing that I have captured their attention, that they have opened their ears and their minds to my words—what a rush!

My passion for words goes beyond vocalization. My first true love burst into my life at seven or eight. I fell madly, passionately, obsessively in love with the printed word, with books.

During my childhood, we never locked our doors. Our nearest neighbors were a quarter of a mile away. We knew and visited everyone within miles of us. One evening as we returned from a mid-week Lenten service we saw a car parked by the back door. Uncle Herman! Our favorite uncle, Mom's younger brother had driven in. He was a seminary student in Iowa and had driven up for Easter break. We charged down the basement steps as he sat up from his nap on the old maroon couch.

Normally I charged into his arms for a hug. But now I was arrested by a towering stack on the kitchen table. Herman caught my gaze. "Ronnie, those books are for you." I approached them slowly. I was drawing near to holiness. Books! Mom had some and the school had some. But books 'for me'? Like the Israelites warily nearing the sacred ark of the covenant, I knew I was entering the sphere of the *mysterium tremendum*.

So began my life-long love affair with reading. That summer I joined the Sugar Creek Gang. Of those 17 books, nine carried me into the world of Big John, Little John, Dragonfly and the rest of the boys. Together we faced robbers, bears and other dangers. I listened to them pray and talk about God. These were Christian adventure books, perfect choices for this pious little Lutheran boy. Maybe Herman's intent in giving me these slim volumes was Christian edification, maybe he was subtly trying to influence my vocational direction. Whatever his motivation, one result is still very obvious. I was then, and still am, overwhelmed by a voracious hunger for reading. The locusts that swarmed through our wheat fields on a dry year needed to eat and keep eating just to stay alive. They devoured whatever plant stood before them and then moved on. Like a ravenous locust I have devoured written words all my life.

Whatever space I occupy—office, bedroom or den—soon fills up with books, magazines, and journals. I read whatever is at hand. The back of a cereal box will do in a pinch. I detest malls but I enter bookstores and libraries as though I were returning to Eden. Why do I read? To step away from the droning din of this life and settle into a world that makes no demands of me. Yes, I admit it, I read to escape. I also read so that I can think new thoughts, so I can examine the world and myself from a different angle. I do not need adrenaline rushes, extreme sports, or living life on the edge. Give me a good book and I am content.

Finally I am passionate about the words I write. When I was in the seventh grade, I announced my career goal: I want to be a writer. I'd wager that not many seventh grade, North Dakota farm boys have ever said that! So, I longed to write. But I longed for other things too. I longed to fit in, to please others, and to 'succeed'. These longings have trumped my first passion for most of my life. Writing is a solitary pleasure. The life of service is not meant to be solitary, nor necessarily pleasurable. And, though writing may bring delight, it rarely brings dollars. Writing sustains my spirit but it does not sustain my family. So, my passion for writing has had to be satisfied with classroom essays, a couple of scholarly articles, a thesis or two, scattered stories, journal entries, letters, and of course, sermons—sermons written by the hundreds over thirty plus years of preaching. My written sermons are strange hybrids—written documents meant to be spoken. I have intentionally cultivated a sermon writing style that is more verbal than literary. All of the things a preacher needs to do in preaching—repeat and summarize, repeat and summarize—all of these quirks show up now in my writing. For good or for ill, I now often write like I preach.

In the beginning was the Word. For as far back into my life as my memory can venture, words have been my passion. I continue to speak and to read with passion. I have been waiting for my writing passion to reignite. The flint has finally found the time and the space to strike the steel.

I was ordained in the spring of 1976 and retired in December of 2013. During my thirty-seven years of ministry I served as an associate pastor at Peace Lutheran in Fargo, North Dakota, as a missionary pastor and evangelist in Brazil, a seminary teacher at the Evangelical Seminary of Puerto Rico, and as pastor of spiritual growth at Messiah Lutheran in Yorba Linda, California. This book grows out of my ministry as pastor, missionary, evangelist, and teacher.

Some of the words in this book have been gathered from the dusty attic corners of my early ministry, some have been sparked only recently. Some tell stories that didn't really happen, but certainly could have, while others try to interpret my ministry experiences. Here you will find essays, short plays, journal entries, a few poems, and several sermons. These pieces defy any attempt at organization. Feel free to open the book anywhere and read what interests you.

All these pieces contain glimmers of my own spiritual wrestling. I am convinced that the spiritual and the material flare into existence together. Every human experience is a meld of spirit and body. This book is a fusion of my flesh and my spirit. These are my words.

2. THE GOOD, THE BAD, AND THE HOLY
(Thinking about ministry)

"Wherever you turn your eyes the world can shine like transfiguration. You don't have to bring a thing to it except a little willingness to see. Only, who could have the courage to see it?" **Marilynne Robinson, <u>GILEAD,</u> page 245**

"Holy Shit!" Over and over again that litany, profane and heavenly, knifed through the shredded clouds. We'd been climbing since seven in the morning. Four teenagers and I were eager to conquer this mountain in the Big Horn Mountains of Wyoming.

Cloud Peak was living up to its name. When we slithered out of our mummy bags at 6:30AM, puffing our breath into the brittle air, the sun was winking off the highest snowfields. By the time we'd eaten our oatmeal and loaded our daypacks, gauzy wisps already were blurring the peak. Cloud snakes writhed down the slopes. The higher we climbed the more often we stopped and gasped the thin air. By now the air we breathed in was as white as the puffs we exhaled. At every rest stop the world grew smaller around us. Sounds disappeared. The chuffing of our breath and the skittering of rocks fell softly into the pillows of cloud. The mountain was reduced to a tight circle circumscribed by five flatlanders determined to reach the summit before noon.

The climb was good—taxing enough to demand all of my energy, even that which I'd lately been spending on frustrating self-analysis. I was two years into my first call as a parish pastor--time enough to recognize that most of the books on my shelf were not central to what was expected of me, time enough to realize that most of my dearly acquired and lovingly cherished knowledge was not exactly irrelevant but was at most secondary to what was needed. And what exactly was needed and expected? Or maybe the right question was: Who in God's name was I supposed to BE among these people? I never had any trouble coming up with something to DO. I could spin out one activity after another, endlessly energetic. No, the crux of my searching wasn't in the doing. It was in the being.

I was troubled by the call to **be** pastor to this congregation. Who was I supposed to be. I hadn't even dared ask myself that question until the past few days. No...the truth was I hadn't seen it clearly enough to ask it until now.

Early in the spring when we began planning, I'd seen this whole youth trip to the mountains as just another activity that would keep the wheels moving, more evidence for anyone who cared to judge whether or not I was doing my job. But since we'd gotten here, something deeper was definitely going on, at least for me. Maybe the piercing alpine air was slicing away fruitless thoughts, or maybe the stripping down to essentials that a week long backpacking trip requires gave me a subliminal incentive. For whatever reasons, during the past few days of hiking and climbing, my mind had gotten to the question and this morning it stood etched in my heart, as clearly as Cloud Peak had cut into the dawn sky. Who was I supposed to be? Huddled at the core of this question was a fear that maybe this call wanted me to be something that I could not be.

But now we were climbing. Breathing, gasping, stretching, and grunting. It was good. At about 11:30AM the trail suddenly ended. Dense clouds gobbled us up. Visibility was no more than ten feet. As far as we could tell, we were on top of the mountain. No trail led upward, and misty cloud swatches came at us from every direction. We may have been on top of the mountain but we could just as well have been in a fog bank back home. We glumly congratulated each other on our 'victory'. Then somewhere out in that white wilderness we heard muffled voices. Deeper disappointment misted our spirits. Not only was all vision hidden, we had not even managed to be the first summiteers of the day. We shuffled, kicked a few rocks with our tired boots and prepared to head back down. Then, suddenly we were caught by that wonderfully profane litany: Holy shit, hooooly shit.

We stumbled toward the strange refrain. The air began to whiten and thin. Luminosity surged toward us, then engulfed us. Like a hurricane peeling away sheet metal, the bold breeze stripped away pieces of cloud. Directly in front of us knelt the shouting hiker, whooping and gasping.

We ran toward him then jerked to a stop. The blazing blue sky, the updraft of cold air, and the vertigo staggered us all. A couple of us dropped to our knees alongside the hiker. Two feet in front of us was chill, frightening, empty air. If you dared peek over the edge you looked straight down two thousand feet to a tiny alpine lake, pale, lonely, and cold in the shadow of the mountain. Lifting your head you could see the short grass plains of Wyoming stretching to the eastern horizon and feel your soul being drawn out of your eyes into its unending loneliness.

Light, cloud, blue beyond blue, goosebump cold air whisking and frisking across our skin. Crazy, beautiful morning standing on top of the world! This truly was some holy shit! Excitement and delight radiated from the faces of my kids. We laughed and shouted for joy and wonder. Holy shit on top of the mountain!

I remembered another mountain, the unnamed one in the gospels that Jesus had climbed, dragging along three of his bewildered followers. Explosions of light, glowing figures, and rumbling clouds had driven the three to their knees. Jesus exploded with luminosity and was suddenly flanked by the Law and the Prophets—Moses and Elijah. A voice boomed from the clouds, "This is my beloved son. Listen to him."

The Bible records the confused offer of Peter (**"Let me build a shelter for us so we can stay here forever!" Mark 9:5**) But what did James and John say? Not a word is remembered. I wonder if they shouted--or muttered under their breath, "holy shit!" That might have been the best way to describe what they had just witnessed. This surely was Jesus, man among men, a creature subject to hunger, sweat, and fatigue, a man just as earthy, as material, as subject to loss and decay as any of them. AND just as surely, this was Jesus hobnobbing with spiritual giants, glowing with transcendence, and being validated by heavenly voices. Whatever this was, whatever HE was, he was also holy, set apart, called out, commissioned for something special. This surely was, **he** surely was, some Holy Shit!

Our adrenalin ebbed and the shouting faded to deep sighs and murmurs. We sat on the stones, ate our granola bars and basked in the glorious freedom that dwells in high places. I looked around at my little troop, my congregation— bursting with brio, so lovely in their joy. What a privilege it was to be here with them. Simply to be part of this experience, to know that even if someday they would forget my name or my face, or even my presence, I still would be with them. Whenever some blue beyond blue hue would catch their eye, or a frisky breeze would nubble their skin, or a distant horizon would pull at their souls, I would be there. I had shared something with them and I'd become part of this group, this body.

Maybe this is what it means to **be** a pastor: To be with people when the shit happens. The good, the bad, and the holy. Yes, especially the holy.
At those moments when the absolute wonder of the everyday is transfigured, when your eyes are suddenly singed by the beauty of the one you've loved forever, when the last breath sets free the *anima*, and you stand at the bedside with the silence thundering in your ears.... When all of that stuff that is of the earth, of the humus,...all of the living and the breathing and the decaying and the dying...when all of that for a moment glistens with the reflected light of God's holy hand...that is where I want to be. O God, what I need most of all is the courage to look intently, lovingly and most of all expectantly at who and what you have put into my world!

3. BREAKING OUT OF BOXES
(A message delivered at the 2007 Messiah Men's Conference)

The year was 1983. I was thirty-four years old. I woke up sweating in the steamy summer air of southern Brazil. No air conditioners, no fans, no screens on the windows. The mangy dogs that ran through the neighborhood had decided to set up a barking contest on the vacant lot next door. My two boys were sleeping in the next bedroom. Josh was six and a half and Justin was three. My wife Lin was sleeping beside me. She was five months pregnant. We planned to have the delivery in the hospital in our little Brazilian town. One doctor, one nurse and a dozen beds. I had accepted a call to be a pastor in the Lutheran church of Brazil two years earlier. That night I lay in bed and through my sweat, I started to shiver. I remember thinking: I am ten thousand miles from home, surrounded by people who don't know a word of English, dependent on one doctor for healthcare, running myself ragged trying to be the pastor to three thousand people, all because of some Jewish guy named Jesus who walked the earth two thousand years ago. Sweating, shivering, dogs barking and I remember asking myself: what if it's all a fairy tale? I am into this Christian business big time, I've put all my chips on this number. What's more, I've got four, almost five people depending totally on me. I'm the dad, the husband, the breadwinner. What in God's name have I done?

Let me tell you, being a Christian man ain't for sissies! Now 'sissy' is a sexist term and if there were any women here I'd be in trouble saying this. Sissy comes from the word sister. To call a man a sissy is to say he's afraid, weak, and timid—just like his sister. Back in '04 Governor 'Ahnold' declared that the state legislators lacked courage and were in fact 'girly men'. They were sissies.

I want to make sure and separate my sister and all sisters from this word. I don't want to get charged with sexism. But if the word "sissies" refers to people who are afraid to live, afraid of conflict or danger or challenge, then I'm telling you being a Christian man ain't for sissies.

Now some of you here might have reason to think that I'm a sissy. About five years ago, I was with a group of Messiah people building a house in Tijuana. On Saturday afternoon, as we were working we heard a guy across the street pounding on the door of a house. It sounded like his wife had locked him out. It also sounded like he'd been drinking. He began to holler at us. "You American SOBs! Why don't you go back home and take care of your own poor people?" We didn't answer and just kept working. So he came over to our work site and got into my face. He pushed me and I backed up. He pushed me again, I backed up again. He was just itching for me to offer some resistance, but I refused to fight.

Was I a sissy? I could have whaled into him or let him whale into me and have had fifteen people covering my butt in a minute. But I didn't. Dennis simply came up beside me and when the man saw his muscles, he drifted away. He evidently wasn't quite as drunk as he acted!

Was I a sissy or not? Would a real man have fought back? How much courage does it take to defy stereotypes? How much guts does it take to break out of the boxes that people try to shove you into? Maybe the sissy is the one who lets the world define who and what he should be.

I've got to admit, or maybe confess, that one thing that most ticks me off is when people try to put me in a box. I get angry when people assume that I must be or think or act a certain way. I am not a preacher's kid. But I am a preacher's grandkid. Everyone in my small hometown knew my grandfather. Many thought he was a special man, almost a saint. Three of my uncles were pastors. And our family never missed a Sunday in church, never missed a church activity. When I was in high school, I even sang in the church choir. My cousin Marvin and I were pushed into choir by our parents. Now I was set up for the sissy label but I did my best to show everyone I was no girly man. I actually became a middle linebacker on our football team mostly because I was a willing to go crazy out on the field. I was willing to sacrifice my body, throw myself at anyone, no matter how big or tough.

I am a farm boy, grew up surrounded by cows, pigs, chickens and wheat fields. I hauled manure in wheelbarrows, drove tractors and grain trucks all through my adolescence. When I went away to college I got put into the dumb, farm boy, hick box. Now, I'll admit, that in many ways I put myself into that one, because I was scared and felt inferior. But it didn't take me long to find out that those cool kids from the big cities could be beaten when it came to tests and grades and I did my best to wax their butts every chance I could. I've just gotta break out of any box that I get shoved in to.

It took me four years of college and one year of grad school in the physics department before I decided that I wanted to be a pastor and I headed off to the seminary. But even in the seminary, people put you in boxes. Those of you who know me know that whatever is set before me I take seriously. So seminary required a lot of reading and writing and by golly that's what I concentrated on. I remember one day someone announced that they were going to have a pick up soccer game. When I showed up, one of my classmates, guy by the name of Gordy looked at me with this sneer and said, "Whoa Baesler, you're here too? I didn't think you were an athlete. I figured you only thought about books." I wanted to give him a cross body block but those aren't allowed in soccer. Don't put me in your box.

After four years of study I became a pastor. I didn't realize how many boxes existed for pastors until I went out to my first congregation in Fargo, North Dakota. I remember pushing my shopping cart down the aisle of the Piggly Wiggly Grocery Store and meeting a little girl and her mom from church. "Look, Mommy, look, its Pastor Ron. Look, he eats too!" Some people, thankfully fewer and fewer, put pastors in the sissy box automatically—non-sexual beings, soft, and wimpish, devoted to life's soft and fine things. Early on, I spent time and energy consciously going out of my way to break down those boxes. Nowadays I mostly just ignore them.

After five years in that congregation, I was invited to go to Brazil as a missionary. Did you know there is a missionary box? I hate boxes of all kinds and maybe I hate the missionary box the most. Another pastor had accepted the call to Brazil at the same time and we were commissioned together at the same worship service and I remember him saying, "Baesler—you're the last guy I'd think of as a missionary." That's because he assumed that all missionaries lived in his box. His box was where we American Christians were superior, the rest of the world was pagan, and our main job was to show these poor slobs how to behave. In his box we were bringing Jesus to a barren land. I despised that box. I might have gotten into Pastor Jack's face about his comments. But at that time Jack weighed over three hundred fifty pounds and tended to spit tobacco juice when he talked, so I just shook my head and walked away. I spent my eleven years in Brazil and my three years in Puerto Rico tearing that box apart, trying to show people that not all Americans were smart, arrogant, know-it-alls, some of us American Christians were willing to learn and grow and serve alongside of them.

Then, in 1998, after seventeen years overseas, I decided to come back and be a pastor in a congregation. I shouldn't have been surprised, but I got blindsided by this one: I got shoved in to another box: the ex-missonary box. Even though by now I had a PHD, had taught in a seminary in Puerto Rico, had worked in rural and urban congregations on two continents for over twenty years, most US congregations that interviewed me figured that because I had been a "missionary" I didn't know enough, I wasn't qualified enough to be a pastor in this country. Let me tell you being shoved into that box was darn depressing.

I thank God for Messiah Lutheran, and for the call committee at that time. They were thinking outside their box and did not put me into some preconceived box either. They interviewed me and decided to take a risk and call me. So, I've had a chance to be the pastor here now for eight and a half years. I'm still working at smashing boxes in the name of Jesus. Believe me, it is not a job for sissies.

That's a small taste of my story. Now lets think about your stories, your lives. You are a Christian man. Like all of us, you are still working out what that means. At work, at school, at home, now that you are retired, now that you are in college, now that you are father or a grandfather. Somewhere along the line, I'll bet that many of you have felt that you were being squeezed into a box. A box made by people who were sure they knew what it meant to be a Christian.

"Oh, you're a Christian? Oooh guys, we gotta watch our language now. Mike here is a Christian." Now I have no trouble with people cleaning up their language. People who use the "f word" five times in a sentence at the very least suffer from an extreme lack of imagination. But some people put Christians into a "holier than thou" box. They assume that because we are Christian men we have this superior, spiritual attitude and we must be judging them, looking down our religious noses at them and condemning them. They put us in a box and resent us for making them feel guilty.

Some Christian guys try to break out of that holier than thou box by showing everyone that they can cuss with the best of them, or be just as wild as the next guy. That can end up looking a lot like life in the men's dormitory back in college. I remember coming home for semester break after living in the dorm with its blue vocabulary. How tough it was to control my tongue!

I don't know about you, but I sure don't feel much holier than the next guy. I'd even argue that a Christian man is a man who realizes just how far away he is from personal holiness. We Christian men see our own sins and know we're not all that holy. Let's not stay in that holier than thou box that people put us in.

Karl was a year ahead of me back in high school. He married one of my old high school girl friends and still lives back in the old hometown. Small towns are great for telling stories and this is the one they tell about Karl. He doesn't go to church. Oh maybe at Christmas or Easter, but that's about it. One day his wife Jan says to him, "Karl, why don't you go to church more often?" He says, "Aww they're all just a bunch of hypocrites in church." Jan said, "Well, you know they always have room for just one more."

That "Christians are hypocrites" box can be a tough one. People look at us, people judge us. They look at how our walk compares to our talk. Or even worse they look at how our action compares to **their idea** of what a Christian should do. Every one of us here has said or done things that we regret, things that we are even deeply ashamed of.

Do we have the courage, the cojones to say, "I'm not a perfect Christian, and I don't pretend to be one. I'm a learner, I am a practicing Christian, and I have to keep practicing because I don't have it down yet." If you can say that, if you can live that, you are definitely not a sissy. It takes great courage to face up to what you really are.

My son Joshua did his first nine years of school in Brazil. He started tenth grade at Roseville Area High School in St. Paul, Minnesota. The first six months of that school year, all he wanted to do was blend in. He didn't want anyone to know that he was different, that he was often confused by high school life. He worked so hard to be just like everyone else.

How important is it for you to fit in, to keep up with the neighbors, to make sure your kids keep up with their classmates? How important is it for you to look at the world just as your friends do?

God has given you men the gift of new life as followers and friends of Christ. Included in that gift is a new set of priorities and values. These don't necessarily match the priorities and values held by your colleagues or your friends. Do you have enough courage to be different? Do you have enough courage to say to yourself and your family what that Old Testament leader Joshua said to his people: "Choose this day whom you will serve. As for me and my family, we will serve the Lord."

The theme for our conference is "Being a Christian Man Ain't for Sissies." Let me tell you how we chose this theme. We had already gotten in touch with our keynote speaker, Kermit Alexander. We didn't know him personally but we knew that he played college and professional football as a defensive back. Defensive backs have to be tough. They have to be willing to throw their bodies around, drive through blockers, and attack runners at full speed. We looked at Kermit the defensive back and Kermit the committed Christian and wondered what the two had in common. We decided that being a defensive back and being a Christian man have this in common: neither one is for sissies. Both of them require courage and strong hearts. Both of them call for a man to give all he has. Both of them challenge a man to the limit. Both of them require men who are willing to break out of the world's boxes.

I want to leave you with the story of man who was not a sissy, a man who in some ways was a lot like us. We meet him in the Bible, in the book of Genesis. The guy's name is Jacob. He's the second oldest son in the family, by a few minutes. His older brother is Esau. Just because Esau got into the birth canal first, he was born with the rights to be the leader of the clan, after the old man Isaac dies.

Jacob is go-getter from day one. He always seems to find a way to get the best of his brother Esau. With the help of his mother Rebecca he manages to trick his dad and steal the rights of the inheritance for himself. Of course when Esau finds out, it hits the fan. Jacob the swindler has to run for his life. He's a crafty guy and he always lands on his feet. You have to admire him for that. Even when he prays he's negotiating! He keeps on the move until he meets some distant relatives, ends up marrying both of the daughters of Laban the richest sheepherder in town.

Twenty-five years later, Laban gets uncomfortable with Jacob's growing power. They agree to split up and once again, Jacob finagles a way to take the lion's share of the flocks and herds. At the same time, Jacob's wives make off with their dad's family statuary. Always Jacob seems to come out on top. But now, without a place to go, he is forced to head back home. And home is where big brother Esau calls the shots. Esau, the brother he snubbed, the brother he despised, the brother he stole from half a lifetime ago.

Jacob does what any savvy survivor would do. He concocts a plan to smooth his return. He sends a whole herd of sheep and cattle, and fine gifts on ahead of his caravan to Esau, thinking he can butter him up, make peace with presents. A few days later, a messenger comes storming into camp, riding a camel all lathered with sweat. He runs up to Jacob, bows deeply and then announces, "Your brother Esau is coming to meet you with four hundred men."

How does that sound to you? If you're riding out to welcome your long lost brother you don't usually bring along four hundred men. What is Jacob the crafty one going to do now? How is he going to get out of this one? When they reach the river Jabbok, he does a really strange thing. He sends all his wives and kids and flocks and herds and servants across the river and he stays alone on the far side. Everything and everyone that is dear to Jacob's now stands on the other side of the river. Everything and everyone that Jacob loves now stands between Jacob and his brother Esau.

Can you imagine Jacob sitting there in the darkness? Some of you have been in the same sort of spot. All his life Jacob has pushed, pushed, pushed. He's had great success. He's done very well for himself. Above the currents of the river he can hear the sheep and the cattle on the other side settling down for the night. He's a wealthy man, a powerful and respected man.

As he sits there in the dark all by himself, what is he thinking? Is he thinking about his own deceptions and the trickery? Is he questioning the priorities that have led him to this dark strip of sand along a lonely river? Is he thinking about how his life has suddenly gotten boxed in? Is he wondering where in this midnight blackness God might be lurking? Or is God riding across the plains with Esau?

I know that some of us have sat there with Jacob. Our chests have gotten tight with fear of the future, with a panicky sense that maybe we're losing control of our lives. Some of us have sat there with Jacob and been forced to face the possibility that maybe we've reached a dead end. We've gotten boxed in by our own way of living.

Jacob sits with his heavy thoughts on the sandy beach. The water sluicing by is the only sound. The silence is suffocating. Then whoosh, out of the night air a figure leaps upon him. He's thrown face first into the sand, he bucks and spins and knocks out the leg of whomever or whatever has attacked him. Who is this creature? Is it a night demon? A nightmare conjured up by his own bleak thoughts? Is it the ghost of his past come to kill him? Is it Esau or God? Jacob fights for his life, gasping, sweating, grunting, this creature will not give in. For an hour they wrestle, two hours, three... His arms, legs are like lead, his grunts become groans.

Finally the sky starts to lighten and the creature sees that Jacob will not give in. So he yanks and pulls Jacob's hip out of joint. Suddenly Jacob has no more leverage, no more spin and buck. The crafty, shifty, powerful Jacob is reduced, and helpless. All he can do is hang on. "Let me go" the creature says. "The sun is coming up." Jacob's lungs burn but his fingers clench the creature and he gasps, "Not until you bless me." And the creature says, "Your name is no longer Jacob the crafty one, but Israel the one who struggled with God and survived." Then the creature blesses him and Jacob releases him.

The sun comes up, this new man Israel staggers to his feet, gets across the river and limps out to meet his brother. Jacob/Israel has learned what some of you men already know and all of you men will one day discover: when God gets a hold of you, the boxes will break, when God gets ahold of you, you may get thrown, tossed, broken. When God gets a hold of you, you will probably get changed, you will very possibly limp in some way or another forever. But one thing you can count on. When God gets ahold of you, you will surely be blessed.

4. CLAY POT PASTOR
(Theological thoughts on Lutheran Ministry)

I was ordained as a pastor in the Lutheran Church in 1976. I was a twenty-six year old idealistic optimist. During the next thirty-seven years that idealistic optimist would more than once become a cynical pessimist. The relentless demands of pastoral ministry, the grinding machinery of ecclesial bureaucracy, and my innate streak of perfectionism—all battered me. I credit my survival to my family, to God's merciful love and to the Apostle Paul. The stories in Acts and his own letters suggest that Paul was a crusty, curmudgeonly fellow. But often his words were my lifeline. Sometimes his words comforted me, sometimes they smacked my self-pitying heart. His words gave me what I needed to continue my labors as a pastor. I especially cherish these words from his second letter to the congregation in Corinth

II Cor 4:1 Therefore, since it is by God's mercy that we are engaged in this ministry, we do not lose heart. ²We have renounced the shameful things that one hides; we refuse to practice cunning or to falsify God's word; but by the open statement of the truth we commend ourselves to the conscience of everyone in the sight of God. ³And even if our gospel is veiled, it is veiled to those who are perishing. ⁴In their case the god of this world has blinded the minds of the unbelievers, to keep them from seeing the light of the gospel of the glory of Christ, who is the image of God. ⁵For we do not proclaim ourselves; we proclaim Jesus Christ as Lord and ourselves as your slaves for Jesus' sake. ⁶For it is the God who said, "Let light shine out of darkness," who has shone in our hearts to give the light of the knowledge of the glory of God in the face of Jesus Christ. ⁷But we have this treasure in clay jars, so that it may be made clear that this extraordinary power belongs to God and does not come from us.⁸We are afflicted in every way, but not crushed; perplexed, but not driven to despair; ⁹persecuted, but not forsaken; struck down, but not destroyed; ¹⁰always carrying in the body the death of Jesus, so that the life of Jesus may also be made visible in our bodies. ¹¹For while we live, we are always being given up to death for Jesus' sake, so that the life of Jesus may be made visible in our mortal flesh.

"We do not lose heart." To "lose heart" means to lose courage, enthusiasm and desire for the task before us or for life in general. During my thirty seven year ministry I pastored congregations, taught seminary students and worked with other pastors. In so many ways we pastors are tempted to lose heart.

Oftentimes we pastors are seduced into thinking that the ministry is our own project or the church is our own property. We then attempt to measure it by our own, or the world's standards. More often than not we are deeply disappointed. We challenge our congregations to action then lament the lack of response. Year after year we preach the grace of God, then sadly discover that our people still live as though they were under the law. We are constantly tempted to measure our own skills as pastors by attendance numbers and by what shows up in the offering plate. Too often our congregations evaluate us that way too. So often we are disappointed.

But we need to keep reminding ourselves that we have this ministry, "by the mercy of God." We need to go back to the cross where the world's expectations are overturned. We survive in the ministry by returning to the cross where all of our notions of success and failure are dethroned.

Paul says the gospel may be 'veiled.' What we call "good news" is not so obvious. This gospel flies in the face of the world's understanding of good news. Sure, there's a promise of life fulfilled. But this promise is grounded on a death and it also includes dying to self and living for others. That's not exactly a grand selling point in today's society!

What's more, vs. 4 says many people are "blind." A blind person cannot "unblind" himself! In order for people to receive this gospel, some outside force need to be at work. It takes many of us pastors a long time to learn this, but the truth is, there are some things that we simply cannot do! Like a farmer we can till the soil and plant good seed. But we cannot produce a harvest. We have no guarantee that our efforts will succeed.

Paul goes on to say that "we have this treasure in clay jars." (vs. 7) We pastors should be clear on what the treasure is. The treasure is the good news of Jesus Christ: the reality that in Christ God has broken the power of sin and death and is working to reclaim his entire creation. This treasure is what we as individuals and we as church have received and share. But what does Paul mean when he says we have it 'in clay jars'?

In Paul's time, clay jars were common, plain, and inexpensive. They are like the simple, unadorned clay pots that we buy today at Home Depot. How are we as pastors, how is the life of our church like a 'clay pot'? The container by which the good news is brought to us and to the world, is **comparatively speaking** worthless. Our personal status, congregational traditions, practices, and programs are as simple and as unimportant as a clay pot. What **IS** important is the treasure they carry: the good news of hope, life, and joy in God's Kingdom.

Let's be honest. It's not easy maintaining the distinction between treasure and container. We pastors find ourselves loving the clay pots of our titles, traditions and programs. Too often we love them as much as, or even more than the treasure. They may not be the best vessels to carry the gospel into the future, but we can't bear to let them go! Even before I was ordained, while I was serving as a seminary intern in a local congregation I saw how easy it is to become enamored with our own clay pots. My wife and I received an invitation to the meeting of the "YA Fellowship." We were informed that "YA" stood for 'young adults' and eagerly anticipated getting acquainted with people our age. We arrived and were shocked to see that everyone there was over sixty! Forty years ago, a group of young people had formed this group as a way to reach out to other young Christians. But they enjoyed their fellowship so much they abandoned the group's mission though they never gave up the group's name. No wonder there were no young adults in the congregation! How many of our cherished traditions are clay pots that we have fallen in love with?

Why does God give us the treasure in clay pots?   Paul says it is **SO THAT** we can clearly see that we are not the owners of this powerful good news. As pastors and leaders in the church we may be "afflicted, perplexed, persecuted, struck down." (What pastor has not experienced those things!) But we are not crushed, driven to despair, or forsaken because, as Martin Luther would say, we are "theologians of the cross." As theologians of the cross we recognize that these afflictions strip us of our pride and ego and move us toward total dependence on Christ. Jesus calls this stripping a type of "dying" to self and says it is actually a way to true life. As we do ministry in this world we "carry in our bodies the death of Jesus." Like Christ's life, our life as pastors (I'd argue the life of all Christians!) is a dying to self for the sake of others. (vs11)   By this dying we move toward the glory of God in the face of Jesus Christ."(vs6) In simplest terms, our ministry is shaped by the cross, it is "cruci-formed."

In, with and under the cross, God is at work. On that Friday in Jerusalem nearly two thousand years ago, in that bloody event, in that actual, agony and death of that solitary man from Nazareth called Jesus, God was changing the destiny of the human race and the entire universe. When we let the cross define our theology then, we are compelled to say this: God uses **finite things** to communicate **the infinite**. Elements in the created order can carry or transmit the love and power of God. This is the basic meaning of the **incarnation** of God in Christ. God communicated divine love and power through the life, death and resurrection of Christ. This is still the way God works today. God uses earthly stuff to incarnate his love: words, bread, wine, water, and the congregation of believers. The very humility of our means deflates our arrogance and dethrones our pride so that in our weakness the power of God is revealed. The tools we have been given to do our ministry—human words, human thoughts, bread, wine, water—are all clay pots.

Most pastors consider preaching to be the central component of their ministry. We spend an extraordinary amount of time and energy in the seminary learning theological terms and their meaning. We grapple with the Biblical languages. We analyze and dissect Biblical texts. We spend hours preparing the Sunday message. Some of us secretly, or not so secretly, take personal pride in our preaching abilities. How often do we realize that the words we have so carefully put together are really only the clay jars? I was forced to face the clay jar character of my preaching early in my ministry.

In 1982 I was sent by the Evangelical Lutheran Church in American to work with the Brazilian Lutheran Church. My first call in Brazil was as a pastor of a parish made up of six congregations with a total of almost three thousand people in a little town called Morro Redondo. I had studied Portuguese for only seven months and now I was preaching three or four times a week. I was speaking at the level of an eight year old Brazilian, maybe even younger. Talk about a humbling experience! I stood up and spoke and every person in the congregation could speak more fluently than I could. After I had been there for three years, Arnoldo, a congregational leader, admitted to me that when I showed up he'd had serious doubts. When I first arrived he asked himself a question that echoed the question of Nathanael in the Gospel of John who said about Jesus, "Can anything good come out of Nazareth?" Arnoldo knew I wasn't Jesus but I was to be his pastor. When I first arrived he'd thought, "Can anything good come out of the United States?" When I opened my mouth it was clear that I was not one of their own. I stumbled over words, used the most basic vocabulary and told simple stories. But here is a crazy fact: more than once in those early years the men and women in the parish thanked me for proclaiming the gospel with clarity! Obviously if the good news reached them, it was not because of my expertise or eloquence.

Those of us who preach are painfully aware of the human character of our words. More than one preacher has heard echoes of what Jesus heard after his first sermon: "good sermon, but wait, isn't this Joseph's son? He played in the streets with our own kids. How can he speak God's word to us?" We pastors can polish our voices, be dramatic and emphatic, we can have our words amplified and transmitted by radio and television, but when we open our mouths and preach, we know. These are human words, our words. No matter the sweat and the theological labor we have put into them, these are our words and when they leave our mouths they are marked with our reality and fragility. If they are accomplishing any of God's work, they doing it by a power other than our own. All of our sermons are clay jars!

I worked in parish ministry for more than three decades. But it doesn't take that long for a pastor to recognize the earthy, clay jar character of Holy Communion. God has declared that the love of Christ, the very body and blood of Christ come to us in the most common of elements. We may use silver plates and cups crusted with jewels but these are nothing but clay jars! I was most struck by this reality on a hot Saturday in my first parish in Brazil.

The little Brazilian community of Morro Redondo was proud to have a tiny hospital. Since I was the only resident pastor in town I made it a practice to visit everyone in the hospital's twelve beds every week. One blistering Saturday as I walked down the hospital's dark corridor a woman called to me. I didn't recognize her. She called me 'Padre', but nonetheless insisted that she and her husband were Lutherans and urged me to enter and see her husband in bed number six. I stepped into the tiny room and was enveloped by steamy, stale air. Two months earlier her husband had had a cerebral hemorrhage and he couldn't talk. He'd been bedridden since then and did not look at all healthy. Frankly, she didn't look much better. She begged me to give them both Holy Communion.

I walked home and got my little portable communion set: a few communion wafers, a tiny tin plate, a bit of wine, two thimble sized plastic cups. I returned, hot and sweaty. Amazingly the beleaguered woman had gotten her husband sitting up in bed. He was leaning against the dingy cement wall, his paralyzed arms flopped limply in his lap. She had to hold him to keep him from tipping over. His hospital gown had slipped off his shoulder and he sat there half naked. I recited the words from my little liturgical book: 'Dear friends in Christ in your weakness and suffering you have desired to receive consolation, patience and peace. You have longed to receive the Lord's Supper." She interrupted my reading with a fervent, "Yes we do!" I invited them to pray with me the Lord's Prayer. She was a large woman, her joints swollen with arthritis. But to pray she insisted upon kneeling on one of the ancient chairs in the room.
So we prayed together the Lord's Prayer. He managed to grunt along, she murmured under her breath. I took out the communion wafers, tiny plate, a small plastic bottle with a few ounces of wind, and the little cups. I balanced them on another rickety old chair that stood beside the worn out cot. Half a dozen black flies buzzed wearily around the room.

Everything was so humble, sad, and pathetic. I pronounced the words of Institution. Did he understand? I gave him a wafer but he couldn't chew it. I picked up the tiny plastic cup and tried to pour some wine in his mouth. Did any go in? Most of it mixed with the saliva that drooled from his mouth. The scene was tragi-comic. If someone had been watching, I'm sure they would have thought it ridiculous. The man almost tipping over in bed, the woman precariously balanced on a chair from the last century and the flies buzzing constantly around us.

I put a wafer made of flour and water into her mouth and said "Body of Christ broken for you." I put a sip of bitter wine into her mouth and said. "Blood of Christ shed for you." I prayed and gave the blessing. The man finally tipped over in his bed. With a great deal of groaning the woman managed to get up from the creaking chair. I gathered up my tiny glasses and plate. As I was leaving, the woman clutched my hand and murmured, "Now I know that the Lord is with us, I can sense his presence and his power." Over and over again as I left, she said, "Thank you, thank you."

I left and walked toward home. I thought to myself: What power? What presence? Did this couple experience anything real? Was it their imagination? If they felt or sensed something it wasn't because of me. If anything, it was in spite of me. I had carried in a couple of communion wafers that were probably a bit moldy and offered two swallows of bitter wine and the same words as always. Everything was so weak, rustic, humble and poor.

The pastor administers the sacraments, proclaims the word. Where is the power? No matter how much gold and silver we put around the bread and the wine, no matter how much marble we put around the water, no matter how high we build our pulpits, no matter how brightly we polish our words, and tout our deeds, we who are the pastors, we know inside ourselves that from **our side** they are all simply bread and wine, water and totally human words and works. We do not own, control, or possess the treasure.

We are clay pots. At the end of my ministry I see this truth more clearly than I saw it at the beginning. I'm a clay pot pastor. I don't need to be perfect, shiny, golden or awesome. What a relief! God manages to use my earthy unflashy plainness to pour God's overflowing love into a desperate world. What a miracle!

5. I WONDER WHY
(A personal challenge)

The assignment: Complete this phrase "I wonder why...?"
I didn't mean to be clever or philosophical, but the first thought that came to me when I contemplated the assignment was this: **I wonder why I have such a difficult time 'wondering why'?** Why is it that I can't savor the question, delight in the mystery, simply hold the wonderful 'why?' in my hand and heart?

The answer is simple: Because I am driven. I am always driven to answer. Being smart is my way of proving my worth. How can I be anyone if I don't know the answer? I have set myself up as the answer man. "Why?" drives me, impels me to search for a solution, a resolution of the tension created by the not knowing. Yes, that's it. When someone asks "Why?" I don't take it as an invitation to ponder together the marvelous mysteries of life. Instead I take it as a challenge to my manhood, humanity, and self worth.

Looking back, maybe that was why I was originally drawn to the sciences. In this realm we can find out. No mysteries here, only problems to be solved. How do we understand the mystery of a frog? Easy. Dissect it, cut it into as many parts as needed, analyze, categorize and label each part. Such is science: divide and conquer. In science, we use knowledge for the sake of control. Of course there is a downside to knowledge as control. In the process of knowing, you kill the mystery. You kill the frog to understand the frog. A dead frog has undeniably lost its frogginess! But I was trained to be a scientist, so when you ask why, I often slip into scientific mode so that I can analyze, critique, categorize and give you an answer. No mystery, no wonder.

But then I left the realm of science and entered the realm of ministry and I discovered another reason for my inability to hold onto that "why" question. Now my reason (or excuse) for hurtling head long to an answer, even a half baked, unsatisfying one, is that as a pastor, people seem to believe that I should have answers to all sorts of questions. Last week, after an evening Bible study, Marla asked me, "Why did God allow John go through so many years of chemo and suffering and die at eighteen?" Instead of speaking the simplest, most honest truth, instead of saying, "I have absolutely no clue at all," I actually sputtered and muttered a few clumsy words. I could rationalize my response by saying that I sensed in her question a deeper 'why': "why is my life so crappy right now?" I didn't want her to think I was brushing her off. Maybe that was at least a part of the dynamic that compelled my response. But I should be honest. I also sputtered shallow theological platitudes because I couldn't allow cracks in my answer man image.

Is it that I am afraid of my own humanity? Is that what it is—this compulsion to come up with answers? Isn't that what tripped up Eve? If you read between the lines of that story, when the snake showed up, it asked her, "Why won't God let you eat from this tree?" Why didn't Eve just say "Because!" and end the conversation? Why didn't she just let it be? Why couldn't she accept her limits and let God be God. But no! She felt compelled to give an answer, to defend God, to justify God. And wasn't her compulsion to answer the question precisely that tiny gap, that little chink in her armor into which slithered the devilish doubting of God's goodness, a doubting that ultimately did her in?

Maybe I will try a New Year's Resolution: Whenever someone asks me one of those impossible "Whys?" I will take a deep breath. Then I will try this response: "What do YOU think?" If that doesn't deflect the question, then I will smile and say, "THAT is a great question! Let's think about it together."

6. NECTARINE STICKERS
(From my journal, August 8th)

My nectarine has a sticker on it with a number, a company's name and the word 'nectarine'. What? Don't they think I know what I'm eating? Of course it's not for me, that sticker. It's for the checkout girl, who scans in the number so her machine can tell her how much of my money she will require before I can leave with my nectarine. It's also for the quality control guy in a big packinghouse so that he can verify that someone has checked out this nectarine before it leaves his jurisdiction. Does a machine do this 'stickering'? I bet not. I think of the poor sticker sticker person—most likely a woman somewhere, bending over an eternal belt of nectarines, tossing the ones that are too small or lopsided or splotched….. All of the unique, different and odd ones are denied a number. They get pitched into a barrel and probably get squeezed out for juice or ground up for baby food. All of the nice ones, the normal ones, the conforming ones—they get stickers, put in boxes, shipped to stores and stacked in bins so we can be sure we're getting great, controlled nectarines.

That is so much like us isn't it, we middle-class, stay inside the lines, don't-rock-the-boat, main line religious folks? We slap normal notes, pass-the-grade stamps, genuine article stickers on everyone that looks like us, acts like us, thinks like us. These are the good ones, the ones we are sure of. No surprises please. You got your sticker? Great, I know how to deal with you. Whoa...what's this? You are stickerless? What happened? Didn't pass the test? Didn't make the grade? Who let you in here? Sorry no room in the inn.

I just feel more comfortable when everyone out there has his or her sticker prominently displayed. Then I know my audience, know what buttons to push, how far to rock the boat, when to back off. I am craving safety and so if I can be assured that all of you have passed quality control then I feel so much more comfortable. Fruit cakes, and nut jobs, screw looses, sad sacks, and *schwermer*— these all make me nervous. People who don't think in straight lines, who zig and zag, or worse, swoop and circle…. People without stickers should all have to sit in one section of the church so I can look over and nod to them once in awhile, keep an eye on them and keep their ideas from seeping in to the rest of this quality assured, smiling crowd.

7. TOUCHED BY THE HOLY
(The pastor's peril)

"Two prisoners whose cells adjoin communicate with each other by knocking on the wall. The wall is the thing which separates them but is also their means of communication. It is the same with us and God. Every separation is a link." (**Simone Weil, <u>Gravity and Grace</u>**)

Imagine you are a technician in a nuclear power plant. Every day you are intimate with frightfully dangerous power, power that could not only destroy you but could ravage the entire world. Yet your heart is not pounding in your throat. You have worked here for a decade. This is your job, your workplace. In the morning you put your brown paper bag lunch in the office refrigerator, then you go out and check the reactors. At noon you sit in the office kitchen, do the New York Times crossword puzzle and munch your apple while the energy of a million suns simmers in the reactors on the other side of the wall.

I have spent over three decades surrounded by the holy. This is my job: Holy Scriptures, Holy Sacraments, Holy Spirit. I am not totally blind and deaf to the presence of the holy. Familiarity has not bred contempt. But I suspect I have become more than a little blasé, even cynical about that mystery we name as "holy," that power we believe is present and active within Scripture and Sacrament. In order to tell you of my experience of the holy, I am compelled to look back in time, to an event outside the boundaries of the Holy Church.

Travel with me to December 30th, 1984. I am exhausted. Christmas is always a hectic season for pastors. But if you are a pastor in Brazil with a flock of 3000 and eight congregations to shepherd, then you can expect a two-week marathon of late night, two hour, home-grown Christmas programs.

The last program had been the night before on the 29th of December at the high walled, whitewashed Capela da Buena, set out on a high hill on the edge of the grasslands. The intense summer heat had forced us to delay the start of the festivities until 9PM. Now at 11PM, a special Christmas choir, self-trained and raggedly rehearsed, was chugging its way through its third musical number. I leaned my head against the organ and dozed off. Finally at 11:30PM I pronounced the benediction, shook everyone's hand and closed down the Christmas season. I drove my dusty, white, battle scarred VW bug home, fifteen miles through the deep darkness of rural Brazil. Thanks to the rocks and potholes in the dirt road I was able to stay awake long enough to navigate home and fall into bed. I looked forward to sleeping in.

Unfortunately, when you are the father of eight and four year old boys and a two year old rambunctious little girl, "sleeping in" is a utopian fantasy. So, on this second last day of the year, I was up with the tribe at 7AM. They were electric with energy because my wife Lin and I had promised them a picnic, or as their Brazilian playmates pronounced it, a 'pickee-nickee.'

By nine AM I was back in the dust-laden Bug, bouncing along country roads. Our neighbor Olvino had told me about a secluded nook along the river. I was looking for a track that wound through the trees and would bring us to the riverbank. "Daddee, Daddee, I see it, right there." Young sharp eyes spied what tired eyes almost missed. We followed the track and parked the car in a glade, dappled with sunlight. A shallow river curved through the meadow and drew the boys like a magnet. Lin had done her usual magic with simple food and all of us laughed, ate and savored the beauty of the day, and the place. After lunch the boys went frog hunting, Lin and the baby lay on the blanket for naps and I walked alone along the river.

I came upon a huge tree that hung out low over the water, bowing like a monk before his bishop. The trunk was broad, nearly flat. It invited me to rest and I lay back on its smooth bark. Beneath me the river chuckled to itself. Above me the leaves gently danced; sunlight and shadow played tag across my eyelids. I felt the tension of the past month, like a clenched fist cramped and aching, slowly releasing and finally opening. I believe I fell asleep, but whether it was for seconds or minutes, I can't say. All I know is that in some wispy territory between waking and sleeping I was struck by—no, that's too violent a word-- I was <u>enveloped</u> by a deep peace. I was acutely conscious of the world around me—the water sounds, the breeze, the dappled sunlight, the trunk against my back—but there was more. "You belong here, all is well." I heard that, or felt that. For an instant, with some part of my being I cannot name, I sensed that I was truly part of this beautiful world. The LIFE that was flowing and giving life to this world was also flowing through me. I was at one with it all—with creation and with this LIFE. For a few moments I was deeply joyful, profoundly thankful, and overcome with an amazing sense of wellbeing. I awoke, stretched luxuriously, began whistling and walking back to my family.

This unspectacular event happened more than thirty years ago. If I could recreate the experience, I most definitely would. I still hunger for the assurance that I belong. I still yearn for that sense that I am truly 'at home.' I crave that sense of unity with God's creation that I savored for a dozen heartbeats. What do you think? Was my experience by the river a brush with the Holy?

A skeptical friend insisted that all of this was just a momentary dream provoked by my exhaustion. I can't prove that it wasn't. He can't prove that it was. Here is what I believe: the holy God was hiding somewhere in that experience. I believe that the peace and joy I felt was my soul delighting in God's quiet nearness. I believe that someday the wall between God and me will disappear and I will delight in God's presence forever.

8. HIKE TO FOSSIL RIDGE
(A poem written in the rocky foothills of Wyoming)

You say nothing ever changes, I say, come with me.

Stand here. Look up. Tell me what you see.

An ancient ocean floor on a limestone surfboard,

Riding west on the crest of a stony Wyoming wave.

How can you say nothing ever changes,

when a mile and a half above the sea

silently looming over you and me

stands a wave paved with ancient sea life

frozen in time, a myriad patinas of lime.

If yesterday's ocean is today's mountain,

then yesterday's Brachiopod is today's voice of God.

"Impatient child, stand here, look up.

Tell me what you see.

The low shall be lifted up, a geological and a biblical thrust.

You too my child shall be made new.

My warrant, my promise, your trust."

9. A MATTER OF TIMING
(A pastor's dilemma)

How much of ministry, and life, is a matter of timing, of fruitfully using the bits of days and scraps of hours before and after meetings, visits and worship services? Given the multiple expectations that congregations have of their pastors, given the exaggerated expectations that many of us have of ourselves, its not surprising that many of us struggle to establish a healthy relationship to time. How does of your struggle compare with this Brazilian pastor's musing?

Strange name for a town: General Câmara. If the town is any reflection on the man, he must have been one of Brazil's least famous generals. General Câmara's main buildings are all the dirty white, plaster-walled boxes common to local military installations—houses, headquarters, and weapons warehouses. I serve a small Lutheran church in General Câmara, a congregation of mostly farm families who have been here for generations. Their lives are ordered by the rhythm of the seasons: planting, plowing, waiting, harvesting and resting. Their time is nature's time. They are neither naïve nor romantic. Nature's time is often capricious and sometimes cruel. Yet they have had to make their peace with it and have to find a way to dwell within it. Occasionally a family from the military base finds its way into our fellowship. Their lives and times are ordered by political expediency, chains of command, and career opportunities. Time is the track upon which their advancement train runs. For the most part it runs alone. There are no grandparents to see their children grow, no cousins to play with their children, no brothers or sisters with whom they can commiserate. How can we bring together in one congregation those whose time is circular with those whose time is so linear?

Even though I grew up on a farm, I am having trouble making friends with this natural time. As a missionary pastor I now find it much easier to identify with those military families. Alone with my wife and children in a huge country, I am usually scrambling to use my time fruitfully. I often feel as though I am fighting time.

From my home in Guaíba to the congregation in General Câmara is forty five miles. But five miles before the town, the road ends at the mighty River Jacuí and I must cope with the Jacuí Ferry. It's a simple, flat-bottomed barge, large enough to haul thirty cars. Every half hour it blasts its horn, belches a cloud of black diesel exhaust, growls out into the current, and cuts across the powerful, half-mile wide river. From my home to the ferry landing is forty miles. Get there on time and you are across in fifteen minutes. Get there a minute late and you must wait. You must wait for it to cross over to the other side, unload, load, return and unload. Timing is crucial. But in Brazil, in most of this world, time is hard to control.

Here is how the journey to General Câmara unfolds: I give my wife Lin a quick good-bye kiss, toss my briefcase onto the back seat and begin my race to the ferry. First I have to navigate the frustrating streets of Guaíba. They are paved with rough stones, stones big and burly enough to bear the daily pummeling of the hundreds of log laden trucks carrying eucalyptus trees to the pulp mill. Those truck tires squeeze up ridges and push down dips. I grind over this sad excuse of a street system and gnash my teeth. My nerves are as rattled as my car by the time I get out to the state highway. Here the pace is faster but more dangerous. For five miles I am in a stock car race down a pot-holed two-lane highway. My competitors are commuters going to and from the capital city, log truck drivers with empty trucks heading out my way for more wood, and log truck drivers with full loads coming at my face. Finally I reach the exit and take the big sweeping curve onto Route 27. Now I've got a straight shot westward on a relatively empty road. I pray that I can make up time, catch up on the minutes I lost on those teeth-rattling cobblestones and on that jammed highway. I clench my jaw, race over hills, dash out into the passing lane, and zip past crawling trucks. Then, just outside of the little town of São Jeronimo, the pavement runs into dust and I square up my shoulders for the last mad dash down toward the river.

Yellow red dust stirred up by passing trucks hangs in the heavy air, too lazy to heed even gravity's law. A few years ago one of my parishioners died in this dust cloud. Carlos and his dad Alberto were on their way to a business meeting, on their way to seal a deal that would make them rich for a lifetime. They charged off the ferry into the dust and met a truck grinding the other way. Carlos was killed instantly. Alberto survived and still lives in his comfortable home in São Jeronimo. But the fragile circuits of his mind have been irreparably cross-wired by the metal plate in his head. He has no sense of time because he has lost all of his memory. Every thought lives for a few seconds in his mind and then disappears. Alberto has only the present moment, no past, no future. Every time I visit him I must reintroduce myself. Our relationship can never grow. Every time I dive into this dangerous dust, I remember Alberto and try to slow down a little. Still, in this race to the ferry, a second savored is a second lost. I peer through the grit watching for the bumper of the last car in the waiting line.

But I am too late. That last car has just inched on board the Jacuí Ferry and it is slowing swinging out into the current. The breeze disperses the diesel smoke and clears the dust. The glistening, powerful river slips silently, relentlessly ocean ward. I will have to sit on the edge of this beautiful, silent river for thirty minutes, and then spend another fifteen minutes riding across. I have forty-five minutes 'on my hands'.

Is this time truly 'on my hands'? If it were on my hands I could juggle it, play with it, and mold it. Why does it feel like it sits on my shoulders, each minute weighing a ton?   I agree that 'forty-give minutes on my hands' sounds more creative and less lethal than 'forty-five minutes to kill'. But, I don't know if I want time 'on my hands' either. It sounds like another burden. What shall I do with forty-five minutes? Work on my sermon, read my book? That question is an echo of a deep inner voice that insists time must be used well and filled up by doing. I suspect it's the same voice that whispers, "You are a pastor as long as you prove you are a pastor, as long as you fill your days with pastoral activities."

The River Jacuí glistens. An uprooted tree glides by like a bedraggled Loch Ness Nellie. Παντα ρε---"everything flows". That was old Heraclitus' slogan. No one can step in the same river twice. Change is omnipresent. Time has you in its hands, whether you like it or not. You may or may not kill time, but someday time will surely do you in.

One of the greatest challenges of Christian ministry is how we structure our relationship to time. For many of us time becomes an enemy. It throws up barriers against which we fling our bodies and spirits. It cuts off every one of our sermons and projects somewhere short of perfection. It reduces too many of our relationships to utilitarian encounters: working lunches, before and after committee meeting chatter. We think, "if only I had more time...."

Those of us who struggle with time need to maintain contact with those who have embraced time or at least signed a peace treaty with it. We must listen to, and learn from those who have been able to "reinhabit time." For me, that means that among other things, I need to visit shut-ins and those who live in nursing homes. They remind me of a different relationship to time.

"The geriatric ward in which so many of our older people now end their days is inescapably full of pain and distress. It would be absurd to pretend otherwise. Yet bound as most of us are by the relentless demands of the clock and the calendar, we find here a world which accepts another kind of time, where requests and reminiscences repeated endlessly remind us of something which the Orthodox liturgy knows with its continual repetitions again and again and again. These people [who] many would prefer to banish and forget, might be speaking to us..of that time outside time of which we need a constant reminder." **(From Ester de Waal's Seeking God, quoted by Kathleen Norris in Cloister Walk, pages 355-6.)**

This time outside our time is God's time. It embraces and surrounds us. Here our time finds its proper place and perspective. Like the ocean, the Dakota plains of my youth, and the ever rolling Jacuí, God's time reminds us of our tininess and our tenuousness. Like the morning mist over this mighty river we rise and disappear. Such a realization can strangle us, or it can free us from the onus of granting a burdensome over-importance to this time and to ourselves.

If the very old can teach us to count our days and not overestimate their importance, then the very young can teach us the preciousness of this moment. Children celebrate the wonder of now. They live "below time". For them,
*"time in the sense of something to measure and keep track of, time as the great circus parade of past, present and future, cause and effect, has scarcely started yet and means little because for a child all time is by and large **now** time and apparently endless."* (**Frederick Buechner, Sacred Journey, page 9**)

My youngest son Toby would give no thought to 'filling' these forty-five minutes beside the river. He would throw rocks, look for fish, smell the flowers, watch the birds, play with other waiting children, and finally be surprised by the blast of the ferry's horn. Time for him is not something that must be filled to justify his existence. Toby's time is eternal not because it never ends but because he embraces each moment as a timeless wonder. Each encounter, event, new day...he does not ponder its origin or fret about its end. He revels in its nowness.

Finally the ferry has returned and grunted back to the dock. I edge onto its rolling deck and am finally on my way to my congregation in General Câmara. Can I remember that these people are a blessing to me? Can I listen to the wisdom of the elders who have learned to count their days? Can I delight with the children as they chase butterflies in the gardens? Will I let God's people teach me how to do ministry and make my peace with Time? God only knows...and time alone will tell.

10. Erich and Friedoldo
(first printed in **The Lutheran Standard**, December 10, 1982)

Senhor Erich belongs to our congregation here in Morro Redondo, Brazil. He and his family are quiet, gracious and kind. They live in a large, beautiful home with all the comforts that might be found in an American home. Erich, a retired banker, is an active member of the congregation and a loyal supporter of the parish programs.

Several hundred yards down the road lives Senhor Friedoldo. He too is a member of the congregation. Like Senhor Erich he and his family are quiet, gracious and kind. But the similarities end there. Friedholdo and his wife and their six children live in a small house with cracked walls and a dirt floor. They have no electricity or running water. Sewage runs in an open ditch past their front door.

Friedoldo is a sharecropper. He works the land of another man. At year's end he gives one fourth of the harvest to the owner. He is surviving but who can say for how long? Friedoldo and his family don't come to church. They are ashamed of their clothes and feel inferior.

To have members from such extremes in one congregation certainly is a challenge to the pastor. But the shocking reality is this: Senhor Erich is the owner of the land Senhor Friedoldo farms. Erich, who has everything he needs, and who faithfully comes to church, regularly collects his quarter share of Friedoldo's harvest. Friedoldo, who lacks everything and stays away from church, keeps his share of the crops and struggles to make it through another year.

Every day we face such realities here in Brazil. Injustices are woven into the fabric of life. What can I say to Erich or to Friedoldo? What responsibility does the congregation have? What if the congregation is divided along "have" and "have-not" lines? How can we address the situation without tearing the congregation apart?

Answers to these questions are elusive, but we have begun with small, practical projects. My family and I have planted a garden. What began as a hobby has become a means of entry into the lives of our people—not only people like Erich, but also people like Friedoldo.

When I come to Friedoldo in my dirty blue jeans with questions about how to plant, I give him a measure of recognition and dignity that he and so many others lack. We spend time with those who have no voice or power. We listen to their fears and their dreams.

And we try to live simply. We walk whenever possible, because then we meet those who have no other transportation. By the way we spend money, dress, and even speak we try to declare our oneness with the least of our brothers and sisters. In our preaching and visiting we challenge both the Erichs and the Friedolos to rethink their roles in a system that benefits the one and demeans the other.

Our congregation owns a small farm. Some members believe it should be used primarily to produce income to help pay church bills. But others see the farm as central to our mission—a place to experiment with better methods of farming for the small producer, a place where people of the land can come together and discover the road to dignity.

The situation in Morro Redondo is not unique. Our national church, the Evangelical Church of the Lutheran Confessions in Brazil, has as its theme for 1982, "God's Earth—Land for Everyone." Through prayers, reflection, and action we have focused on the injustices of land distribution and use. We have discovered that we really are dealing with a world-wide situation in which the often well-meaning Erichs live oblivious to the suffering they inflict on their neighbors, the Friedoldos.

The problems are global. But no global solutions will be found unless we are willing to tackle the concrete, local realities. So, here in our corner of Brazil, we will keep working our garden, walking alongside the poor, and sharing the good news that promises wholeness to all of God's children.

Believers in communities around the world are called to do the same, wherever Erichs and Friedoldos live side by side, yet so far apart.

11. FOUR NOTES FROM BRAZIL

November, 1981

We've been in Brazil for almost a month. If I were to describe what is happening to us now, I would begin by telling you about "our" rooster. We live on the fourth floor of an apartment building. Next to our building is a vacant lot surrounded by a ten-foot high cement wall. Tucked in the corner of the lot, right next to our apartment building is a little house. A family lives there, unnoticed by everyone but those of us who can look down into the lot. This family has some chickens---and a rooster. This rooster does what all good roosters do, he crows. And his is a robust, full-throated, "I'm in charge" kind of crow. His timing is superb. At five AM before any other rooster, not to mention any bird, dog, or person, is awake, this rooster breaks forth with a crow that assaults the night and imperiously summons the sun. He persists until the sun responds. I am living in Brazil and now I must live with that rooster.

Moving to, and settling in to a new country is like that. We come eager for newness and changes. We welcome the opportunity to taste and feel how life is lived in another corner of the globe. And, yes there is much to delight in, much to savor and enjoy. But there is always that rooster! There are always those customs that challenge deeply held beliefs, those peculiar perspectives that seem totally foreign, or those irritating circumstances that challenge cherished living patterns (like sleeping peacefully past five AM!) Then we must decide what to hang on to, what to give in to, what to put up with, what to resist. We begin to understand that our new country is also part of the broken world. We begin to see that some of the changes will not be pleasant and may need to be fought against. We begin to love the country and the people for what they are, instead of what we imagined they would be. After one month in Brazil, that is what we are doing: learning to live with, and maybe even love, that rooster!

March, 1983

This is our first Easter season in Brazil. The children are going back to school after summer vacation. Some of the corn has been chopped for silage. The rest stands in the fields, whispering and drying in the cool wind. Pumpkins and melons lie like smooth stones in the fields. The plants are losing their bright green. Fall is coming to southern Brazil. And we are getting ready for Easter. The northern half of the globe can talk about Easter and new life blossoming, Easter and new hope budding. Northern Christians can celebrate Easter along with the death of winter and the birth of spring.

We in the southern half of the globe are not as tempted to see Easter as one aspect of the eternal cycle of nature. Here in southern Brazil nature is not cooperating with us. Or rather, we are not cooperating with nature. The days slowly weaken and the winter rains will soon begin to fall but we stubbornly insist on new life, not the new life budding from the ground, or blossoming in the trees, or bleating in the barnyard. That really is not new life; it is the same kind of recycled life year after year. We stubbornly insist upon celebrating a new life that breaks the old cycle of death and decay, a new life that comes as a shock and a surprise. Easter is about the new life that only God can bring. It is about a new life that can move us to dream, dare, and even die, because it promises that beyond all winters and summers, beyond all plantings and harvestings, there will be true life forever.

July 1983 (reflections after a pastoral visit)

Impossible Paulo! Impossible. All of your life spent on these weary, rock-strewn acres. All of your twenty-four years spent striding across this too-weak-for-weeping soil. All of these years hiding from the winter wind in that little box of crude bricks. Parents, brothers, sisters and now you, your wife and your daughters, all nine of you breathing together that stiff, acrid smell of dirt and smoke.

Impossible Paulo! All of your life lived here on the shoulder of this giant. All of your twenty-four years lived in the shadow of this warm, wild, green mountain. All of those years with this deep pile carpet of palm and eucalyptus stretching up and beckoning you, right outside your door.

We are walking across one of his fields. Paulo stops his striding. His eyes climb the lush slope. The winter wind snatches at his hand-rolled cigarette. "That there is the highest point around here." His pale blue eyes lose themselves in a far country gaze. "They say up there on top there's a flat space big enough for a field." He draws on his flimsy cigarette. "I wouldn't know. I've never been up there." His bare, leather-hard feet renew their striding. I follow, but behind me I hear the giant whispering, wild and lonely.

Impossible, Paulo! Impossible. Where is the little boy who had time to be a little boy? What happened to the animal curiosity of the child? What happened to the adventures of brothers and sisters, world explorers, jungle penetrators, new land discoverers? What has poverty, sadness and frustration done to you Paulo? You shall one day be laid down in your too-weak-for weeping soil never having seen the world from the top of your very own mountain.

February, 1986 (Lenten self-examination)

Here in Esteio, in this urban area in southern Brazil, some people live on the garbage of others. Before the city can pick up the bag of my household garbage, a man in a horse cart hastily grabs it and takes it to a vacant lot. There it joins thousands of other bags, is torn open and dumped onto the ground. Men, women and children scramble to dig through it, looking for things to eat, use or sell. What is garbage to me, is gain to them.

My congregation has not reached out to these people. Very few Lutheran congregations in Brazil have made any concerted effort to minister to them. Even fewer congregations have tried to bring these people into their fellowship. As I ponder the reasons for this, I'm drawn to the Apostle Paul's words in his letter to the Philippians. ***For Christ's sake I have thrown everything away; I consider it all as mere garbage so that I may gain Christ and be completely united to him****.* Everything that gave him status in this world—his ancestry, his knowledge, his correct behavior—all of this and more Paul threw aside so that there would be room in his life for Christ.

Why don't we as a church reach out in compassion to these "garbage people?" Could it be that as a church we are too full, full of our own ethnic pride, our doctrinal purity, our good name? Do I dare be as bold as Paul and call these things garbage? If these things clutter up our congregational life so much that we can't respond to the crying voices around us, then surely we must reconsider their value. Or, could it be that as citizens of a 'developing country' our personal lives are too full, full of "look out for number one, every man for himself, every woman for her man, buy, invest, grow, don't ever look back"? Do we dare be as bold as Paul and call these things garbage? When we consider how these ideas fill our lives and blind us to the misery around us surely we must reconsider their value.

We as individuals and as a church aren't reaching out to the garbage people because we are desperately clinging to OUR precious garbage. Paul said to the Philippians, ***All I want is to know Christ and to experience the power of his resurrection, to share in his sufferings and to become like him in his death, in the hope that I myself will be raised from death to life. Philippians 3:10***

As long as we insist upon clinging to our precious garbage, we will not be able to move out and know Christ as Paul sought to know him. We will not be able to walk openly and care-freely into the places where Christ suffers with his people. And we will not experience the power and beauty of the new life that only Christ can create out of that suffering. Certainly that would be tragic. But more tragic still would be the fact that these men, women and children would continue to live alone on our garbage.

12. TEN YEARS IN BRAZIL
(From a letter to US Lutheran congregations)

October 4, 1991

Dear Friends in Christ,

Today marks one decade here in Brazil! Ten years of being missionaries of our Lord, ten years of experiences which have indelibly marked our lives.

One such experience happened within our first week in Brazil. On a beautiful warm evening we went out for pizza. We sat around a table on the patio of the restaurant savoring the tropical atmosphere. When our pizza arrived, I picked up a huge piece, so thick with cheese the crust was sagging. I readied my eager, saliva laden mouth. Then I noticed the children peering over the low wall around the patio: hungry eyes, hungry faces, hungry little bodies. I looked around at the other customers. They ate and chatted without a glance at the ragamuffin troop. I looked at the size of the pizza, looked at my family and at the number of children outside the wall and I admit, I confess, that I lowered my eyes and ate my pizza.

That was ten years ago. Unfortunately the plight of children here in Brazil has, if anything, worsened since then. We are witnessing with horror the headlines of a new crime: the assassination of street kids. These are children and teenagers who've been abandoned by their parents, or whose parents have died. They survive by petty thievery, begging, or selling fruit on the streets. On average three such children are killed every day. One businessman in Sao Paulo said, "Eliminating these street kids is good for society." That may sound shocking but within the terrifying logic of our system it makes sense. On an average day here in Brazil, one thousand babies die from hunger or preventable diseases. A savage, dog-eat-dog capitalism, widespread corruption in health services and a government more interested in self preservation than national well-being all work together to assassinate these babies. Shooting a ten-year old street kid who sleeps in the park and lives by petty thievery is just a logical next step in the process. Eliminating a threat to ones profits and ones safety without spending any money— what could make more sense in a reality governed by profit and self-interest?

In the Gospel of Mark, Jesus says, **"Whoever receives one such child in my name receives me." (Mark 9:37)** What might it mean to 'receive' one of the world's small victims? Does it mean risking fleas and head lice? Opening up your home and your pocketbook? Living with more confusion than you'd like? Can you do that?

36

Our Brazilian national church has several programs for working with street children, one of them was begun by an ELCA missionary. Our congregation here in Guaiba supports a day care center that allows mothers to work and help support the family and keep children and parents together. Perhaps your congregation also is doing such things. But before we start patting ourselves on the back, let's reread Jesus' words: Whoever receives one such child in my name receives <u>me</u>. Receiving one of the world's victims is more than an act of charity or a good work that pleases God. Receiving one of the world's victims is related to our receiving Jesus. It is related to our salvation.

The disciples had trouble with that. Brazilian Christians have trouble with it. American Christians do too. Who wants to be part of a movement that identifies itself with victims, with losers? What we want is success, profit and security. This man who kneels down and hugs a runny-nosed street kid—how can we call him Lord? We want a Lord who is well dressed, well behaved, someone who moves comfortably in our safe circles. This man with an urchin from the street in his arms...Mercy! He's probably already picked up head lice!

No, we are certainly not pleased with this. But Christ does not come to please us. Christ comes to save us, save us from our pride and our self-centeredness, save us from our fears and insecurities. Do you want to open your life to this Savior? Then receive one of the world's victims. Look into the eyes of this sufferer, feel his pain, listen to his story, see the hope s/he clings to. Leave behind your dreams of greatness and success, leave behind your preoccupations with yourself. Make room in your life for the other—and Jesus too will enter in.

13. What Should We Do With All These Beans?
(A ministry surprise)

Six scruffy boys from the neighborhood gathered around the full burlap sack. "What should we with all these beans?" Ten months ago, who would have dreamed they they'd ask that question? Ten months ago who could have predicted the answer they gave?

Everything started when Albertina and Elza, two widows who live in the shantytown not too far from our parsonage in this southern Brazilian town, complained to me that the kids just "run around and get in trouble." We discussed that complaint and finally realized that these kids had nothing to do but get into trouble. One mother suggested, "Why not try a community garden?" Someone offered us a vacant lot, a farmer offered us bamboo for a fence, the congregation took up a special offering to buy seeds. Now the trick was to link up all of these resources with the energy of the neighborhood kids. This was no easy task. Working together on a community project is a new experience for most people here. These kids were growing up in a feudal society where you only work for the boss, where the boss 'takes care' of you and discourages initiative. The kids, like their parents had a hard time seeing the value of a community project. But the soil was prepared. The very same two widows whose complaint had started it all kept hoeing and inviting. Finally on Brazil's Independence Day (September 7th) six of us started to cut bamboo and drag it a quarter of a mile to our garden. Before long a few more kids showed up, then more. Soon a bamboo brigade of fifteen was huffing and puffing across the fields. At noon, the four adults decided to quit for the day. But three boys asked me if they could come back and work in the afternoon. Maybe a new seed was sprouting.

Within a few days the fence was done and the seeds planted. During the days of waiting, interest in the garden waned. Once again it was Albertina and Elza who kept things going—hoeing and fussing with the seedlings. But the kids seemed to have lost interest. They never showed up unless I did. I began to wonder if it was all worth the effort.

Then in early December the green beans started producing. "Come on gang, let's pick beans." A rag-tag gang of six boys piled into our white VW for the two block journey to the garden. Within a half hour the potato sack was nearly full of beautiful long pods.

"What should we do with all of these beans?" they asked. Alesandro remembered our first rule: Whoever works in the garden has the right to pick and eat. So we stopped at the tiny homes of Albertina and Elza and brought in beans. Then we stopped at each boy's little shack and filled a basin or pot. But the sack was still nearly half full. "What should we do with the rest?" I asked. Then little Davi, the rascal who threw a stone at Albertina last week, little Davi with the runny nose and ragged shirt, little Davi looked at the beans and at his buddies and declared, "I know! Let's give them to the poor!"

And so we did! My six little friends, whom I considered poor, directed me to homes where people needed vegetables. They gave away their green beans with great joy and energy. Somehow they had learned something very important. They had learned to see the needs around them and respond generously. They had done a very Christian thing. Yet many of them have very little contact with the church.

We hold services regularly in their neighborhood and will soon be offering a week long Bible school there. But Davi and his friends aren't very active. Yet somehow a seed has been planted in their lives. In the midst of dragging bamboo, hauling manure and working alongside Elza and Albertina the Spirit of living Christ has begun to work. I've learned something too from my ragamuffin friends. We do not "spread the Gospel" to the pagan world. God's Spirit spreads that Good News. We are his instruments, humble and often unwitting tools in God's worldwide mission.

14. HOW WILL WE RECOGNIZE EVIL?
(A theological reflection)

Finally, be strong in the Lord and in the strength of his power. Put on the whole armor of God, so that you may be able to stand against the wiles of the devil. For our struggle is not against enemies of blood and flesh, but against the rulers, against the authorities, against the cosmic powers of this present darkness, against the spiritual forces of evil in the heavenly places.
Ephesians 6:10-12

This Brazilian night air felt unusually heavy. I coasted down the long hill on the dirt road slashed through the somber jungle and stopped my dusty VW in front of the tiny church. It was obvious that something in this Saturday evening worship gathering at Arroyo Moreira had been altered. Ordinarily, the men would be standing in a circle in front of the door, talking about fields and milk cows, laughing at the local politicians and puffing on hand-rolled cigarettes that glowed like the fireflies in the bamboo grove beside the church. Ordinarily the children would be running and shrieking, playing tag and other games whose names I did not yet know. Ordinarily the women, wise in the ways of making the most out of little, would be sitting inside on the simple benches closest to the church door, waiting for the last faint night breeze, resting their tired legs and catching up on family news. Ordinarily everyone would wait for the pastor to coast down the hill, unload his car, put on his clerical robe and then, only then everyone would unhurriedly move their fellowship into the small whitewashed church and prepare for worship.

But tonight I climbed out of my dusty VW bug, walked up the brick path with my robe over my arm and stepped into a church full of quiet people, not peaceful quiet, but coiled spring quiet. The humid atmosphere hummed with an invisible energy. The only sounds were the muffled barking of a dog behind the bar across the dirt road from the church and the constant hissing of the gas lantern, our only source of light which hung from a wire above the center of the aisle.

I didn't dare to ask the obvious question. I was still too much of a stranger in their midst and I didn't want to offend. Days later I discovered that only minutes before my arrival in the dusty street in front of the church, Rui, the congregation's treasurer and Raul, another church council member, had gotten into a blistering argument. It ended with each one throwing a couple of punches and then being restrained by the other men.

When the congregation heard the sound of my little car winding down the mountainside in the still of the evening, they all slipped inside, ashamed and embarrassed. I didn't know this as I began the evening worship service. But something had shifted, that much I could feel. Some fault line had shuddered and, as I soon discovered, a chink had been opened in our fellowship, a chink through which more than one dark surprise would enter.

I had barely begun the liturgy when through the open door I saw a man coming up the walk out of the darkness. He stopped for a moment in the doorway. Then, with arms upraised he began wobbling down the aisle. He stopped directly in front of me, arms still elevated and he slurred, "I want to talk to you pastor." His last port of call had been the tiny bar across the street. His breath told me that much. "I want to talk to you pastor, " he loudly insisted. I quietly whispered, "We're in the middle of a worship service. Why don't you sit here and join us and then after the service we can talk." Amazingly he nodded and sat down in the first pew, which in good Lutheran tradition was empty.

Back to the liturgy, a hymn and the bible reading. I had just begun the sermon when Enilda, a woman sitting in the midst of the congregation stood up. Her eyes were huge and dark. She pushed her way out of her pew, ran up the aisle to the door, paused and opened her mouth. From some place of pain, some deeply wounded place came a wail, an ear shredding shriek. Then she turned and stumbled down the stairs into the heavy purple night. Her husband and half of the congregation stampeded after her. By the time I made my way down the aisle and out the door she was sitting in the rough grass beside the walk, crying quietly in her husband's arms. "It's OK pastor. She'll be all right. She's having some problems with her nerves. We'll just walk on home. We're OK." They slowly plodded up the hill. Their neighbors and friends whispered in the hushed night. I wondered if they were less shocked than I by Enilda's outburst.

Whether I was a wise or a foolhardy shepherd that night, only God knows. At least I was persistent. I urged everyone back inside, led another hymn and began my sermon again, from the beginning. I can't remember what I said but I remember that I preached with half-held breath, as though a tight cord surrounded my chest. Only with the "Amen" did it loosen a bit. Before the closing prayers the congregation shared its community announcements. I was eager to share my news. "The Bibles you ordered have finally arrived. You can pick them up right after the service." Raul, a church council member but one who rarely came to worship, stood up near the back and announced, "After the service, the church council will meet." Strange, I thought. Why doesn't Walter, the council president make that announcement? But Walter, who was quite deaf, sat oblivious in the second pew.

Finally, thankfully, the last hymn was sung and this singular service was over. But the tumult had not subsided. Just the opposite! Our friend from the bar immediately clutched my robe, eager to talk. The half dozen people who had waited for months for their new Bibles accosted me, eager to pay and get their hands on the Word. And what had been announced as a council meeting was in fact only a slightly more civilized version of the fist fight that had begun the evening. From what I could overhear it was an argument about church contributions and like a fast approaching tropical storm, the mutterings were mushrooming into roarings.

At last, after dealing with the checklists and the change-making, I distributed all of the Bibles. Now the man from the bar sensed his opportunity. But he couldn't understand my rudimentary Portuguese and I did even worse with his slurred words. The turmoil brewing among the leaders in the corner, not to mention the tumult in my heart, was sweeping away my capacity for compassion. In a wobbly huff, the visitor from the bar, tottered out the door, muttering about this new pastor who didn't want to communicate. I confess I was relieved.

By now the thunderclaps from the council "meeting" filled the little church and the storm seemed destined to crass upon us all. Then, taciturn, nearly deaf council president Walter decided that he had heard enough and seen enough. He walked into the center of the circle of antagonists and said in disgust, "The lantern is mine and I'm going home." He grabbed the gas lantern from its hook, turned it off and stalked out the door. We stood disconcerted in the darkness. In the sudden hush, we could all hear the men's angry breathing. The vast blackness of the tropical night poured in through the door. In the darkness we finally all could see, see the pettiness of the argument and the futility of the whole evening. I quietly murmured, "Friends its eleven o'clock. This night has not gone well. Let's follow Walter. Let's go home."

I ground up the dusty hill in my VW and wearily drove home. What had just happened? What had gone wrong? Was evil there and how had it shown itself? Was evil localized or was it somehow above and within everything that had gone on? Had Rui and Raul's violence ripped a hole in the fabric of the community, a tear that allowed the "spiritual forces of evil" to disrupt our worship of Christ the Lord? How was Enilda's outburst related to the "cosmic powers of this present darkness"? Our inebriated visitor, was he a vehicle of these forces, or its victim, or perhaps both?

I bounced over the rocks and ruts and replayed the night's events, this time against the backdrop of the larger world. Every one of the people gathered in that little church is a subsistence farmer. Not only are they dependent upon the capricious weather, they depend upon capricious marketplaces whose prices were determined by men in offices far from their valley. These distant men probably are no better or worse than the farmers, but they are bound to a system whose ultimate criteria isn't human well being but profit margin.

Many men, including some of our members, try to forget the precariousness of their situation through cane whiskey, like the night's visitor. All of the people gathered there shared in one degree or another a sense of powerlessness. With that reality in mind, it's no surprise that a member's contribution to the church could be a point of conflict. This contribution raises serious personal questions, economic and spiritual questions. Personal jealousies, egocentric competition, inferiority complexes, pecking order issues—all could certainly crystallize around the matter of church contribution.

As I traveled the last miles through the jungle and approached the parsonage, I reflected on the fact that none of those people gathered there tonight possess any great power to change the social political reality. A military government has ruled this country for decades. To an outsider the church council looks like a very feeble, inconsequential organization. For those people in that tiny church it represents one place, maybe the only place where they can exercise any power. What models for the healthy exercise of power do these people know?

All of the people in my little church lack access to health services. Enilda works long hours in the fields, eats enough to fill her stomach but not enough to fill her protein and vitamin needs. She never sees a doctor, and spends nights haunted by the future she sees for her children. Was her cry triggered by my sermon, her nightmarish fears, a sudden vision of life's futility, or her fragile nervous system?

I parked my dusty little car in the garage and quietly entered my hushed home. How insidiously evil creeps into life. It became clearer and clearer to me that tonight I witnessed the personal expression of the dark spiritual powers. Tonight the chaos of evil worked to disturb the community of hope. That battle continues in the daily lives of my people. I pledged that in our next worship gathering we would reengage the battle as a community of believers. We will persist, resist and proclaim, until every knee will bow and every tongue confess that Christ is Lord.

15. NOW THEY HAVE KILLED THE RICH MAN'S COW
(Solidarity with the poor)

I stood before my little Lutheran congregation in southern Brazil. "We have a guest with us today. Ademir, will you please stand up." A slim man stood. He was blushing and looked at us with a shy grin. I spoke to my parishioners. "I know that you have all heard about the Sem Terra people. The newspapers and the TV people have said all sorts of things about them. Does this young man look like a dangerous radical to you?" They smiled sheepishly.

Ademir was a blond, thin twenty-year old Brazilian, and like most of my congregation, he was of German descent. He had been the president of the youth group in the country congregation where he used to live. His father was a landless farm worker. The tiny house they lived in was their own. The tiny plot of land around it belonged to them too. But the land the family cultivated and sweated over was not their own. They were sharecroppers. Sharecropping is always a low-return effort but when the price of soybeans kept dropping while prices of fertilizers and pesticides kept rocketing upward, Ademir's family began to wonder if it was all worth it.

Finally they decided to join the Movimento dos Sem Terra—The Landless Farm Workers Movement. This group has been struggling for decades to promote a redistribution of land in Brazil, where vast tracts of land lie unused, held by state and federal governments or owned by wealthy city dwellers as a hedge against inflation.

The Movement keeps before us all the will of God as expressed in Psalm 24: "The earth is the Lord's and the fullness thereof." If the earth is the Lord's then the earth does not exist primarily to guarantee wealth for the already wealthy. If the earth is the Lord's then the earth exists to sustain and give life.

But Ademir and his family discovered that the will of the Lord meets with tremendous resistance in a world accustomed to making its own rules and guaranteeing its own privileges. Despite the fact that land reform is explicitly written into the Brazilian constitution, despite the fact that millions of acres of arable land lie untouched, despite the fact that all major cities are already surrounded by slums full of people who have left the rural areas---despite all of this, the landless poor who want to work and produce food for their families and their country are resisted every step of the way.

Ademir and his family spent two and a half years living in a tent made of black plastic. They camped alongside a federal highway with thousands of other families. They participated in public protests, meetings, conferences, pilgrimages and marches to the state capitol. They did what they could to force the government to keep its promises.

Of course they were portrayed in the media as "anarchists, communists and lazy bums who want something for nothing." Very few people in Brazil believe that any group can organize and change society. Those who do organize and push for change pose a threat to the cynics and so must be discredited lest the rest of society be put to shame. Add to that the tremendous power of the rich landowners who benefit from the status quo and you begin to see how difficult any land reform can be.

But Biblical stories, like the Exodus narration of God's people seeking the promised land, continue to inspire the Movement. Sheer persistence sometimes pays off. On December 9, 1991, Ademir and his family, along with thirty other families, were finally resettled on eight hundred acres of state owned land next to our town of Guaiba, Rio Grande do Sul.

Their victory was bittersweet. As a last act of vindictive violence, the state police confiscated the farmworker's tools when they left their campsite along the highway. They arrived in Guaiba with their black plastic tents, their families and little else. The government had promised them food to keep going until they could harvest their first crops. But the promises were not kept. They worked hard, planting when they could get seed, even though it was very late in the planting season. They dug a well by hand. They received with gratitude what local churches could provide.

They faced another challenge. A rich local rancher continued running his one hundred and twenty head of cattle on what was now their land. Finally, in desperation they penned up twelve of his cattle. When the rancher showed up they told him, "Look, we don't want to hurt your cattle. We are doing this to call the government's attention to our plight. It's a form of protest."

The rancher seemed agreeable. He said, "I can see you are suffering. I sympathize with you. I'll even donate a cow for you to butcher."
The farmers protested. "Butchering a cow will solve our problem for only a few days. The government promised to give us enough food to see us through to harvest. We want the government to keep its promise to us. If you want to help us, join us in our protest."

Now it was the rancher's turn to protest. "No, I can't do that. You see, I've run my cattle on this land for many years without paying rent to the state. I can't call attention to myself without getting into trouble."

The discussion went on past sunset. The desperate hungry people and the rich rancher were at an impasse. The rancher finally jumped into his pickup and left. In frustration the farmers decided to accept his offer of a cow. By the light of a bonfire they killed one of the cows and started dressing it out.

Suddenly, in the middle of the butchering, sirens blared, lights flashed. The rancher had returned with the police. Ademir and twenty other men were rounded up, their wives and children were terrorized. Eleven men spent the night in jail and were released pending a hearing. Was this a set-up? A trap? A misunderstanding? Why didn't the TV and newspaper report that the slaughtered beef was divided up and kept by the police?

Ademir and his family don't know the answers to these questions. But Ademir tells us he is sure of one thing. "Getting arrested and getting harassed ---that's just what happens when you struggle for justice and dignity."

This event left the members of my congregation uneasy. They were willing to donate used clothes and food to the new settlers. "But now they have killed the rich man's cow. They have disobeyed the law of the land and challenged the authorities." Beneath their uneasiness lies an unspoken question: "Do we dare stand in solidarity alongside these people who do not submit to the corruption and indifference of the government?"

A few days before Passion Sunday our women's group went out to the farmer's settlement. We walked in to the camp on the muddy paths. We sat on logs outside the ragged plastic tents. We met with our newest neighbors. We listened and asked questions. We shared our faith. We pondered together what it means to carry the cross in a belligerent, selfish world. Together we reflected upon the cross of Christ whose death marked the ultimate act of solidarity with suffering people.

The story of Ademir and the others in this new settlement is still being written. Their story, in all of its many variations, is unfolding around this aching planet. As a disciple of Christ, whom will you support? With whom will you stand?

16. CHOOSE THIS DAY WHOM YOU SHALL SERVE
(Thinking about religions)

Now if you are unwilling to serve the Lord, choose this day whom you will serve, whether the gods your ancestors served in the region beyond the River or the gods of the Amorites in whose land you are living; but as for me and my household, we will serve the Lord." (Joshua 24:15)

6:30AM I step out of the parsonage as the sun rises on another day in southern Brazil. The morning breeze tickles the waters of the River Guaiba, three miles wide here on its serpentine journey to the Atlantic. My feet crunch through the sand, my heart reluctantly begins to wake up, lazy muscles stretch. On my morning run I pass driftwood, the usual plastic jugs, cans and bottles. Then, suddenly, as if budding from the sand itself, three goat heads grin up at me. Instinctively my legs and my heart leap, and high-octane adrenaline launches me down the beach. I slow as a come to another more common sight: plates of fruit, candles, and bottles of cane whiskey. What is spread out here on the beach this morning, and nearly every morning is not the remains of a late-night lover's picnic. These fruits, candles and alcohol, as well as the three shocking goat heads, are offerings made to one of the gods of Umbanda, a rapidly growing Afro-Brazilian religion. In Umbanda, spirit messengers of the gods possess mediums and through them give advice and counsel to those who come for help. Sometimes the spirits, speaking through the medium, suggest to the seekers that their personal problems could be resolved by a sacrifice of some sort to appease or delight a divine being. The articles I encountered on my morning run were offerings made to gain a god's favor.

Umbanda participation is not limited to one race or class. Some who belong to the Roman Catholic Church or one of Brazil's many Protestant churches come to Umbanda's nighttime gatherings. I am told that some of my own congregation's members can be seen there too, and that one of my parishoners even participated in a marriage ceremony at an Umbanda center in a neighboring town. We live in a chaotic threatening world and people of all classes are tempted to appeal to any and all gods for help.

As I slog through the sand alongside the river, I consider these gods and the God whom I worship. Was there ever a time when it was different? Jesus was not born into a neutral god-less world. How often have I sung, "O little town of Bethlehem, how still we see thee lie. Above thy deep and dreamless sleep, the silent stars go by." But I wonder, was Bethlehem's sleep really so deep and dreamless, untouched by the threats of hunger and pain? Were there no fears that haunted its slumber, no nightmares of death, no wrestling with angels, no groaning for a sign from a god, any god? The Roman Empire of Jesus' time was not a godless vacuum waiting to receive a new deity. It was a world already overpopulated with divine beings. Already in his first months of life, Jesus had to be hastily wrapped up and carried across the border. He had to flee from those whose gods where threatened by his presence. Jesus did not land placidly on a peaceful, dreamless, god-empty planet. Jesus, helpless babe, God's love incarnate, came into a troubled, restless world as a challenger and a threat to the many gods of the land.

Every day as I run on the sandy beach I am challenged by someone else's gods. As Joshua reminded his people as they prepared to enter the Promised Land, this world is full of options, and people have choices to make. Sometimes the options are clear: Oxala, head of the Umbanda pantheon, OR Jesus the Christ. Sometimes the options are not so clear. "I am a religious person, I have my faith. I'm a Christian and I pray. But I can't sense any need for this congregation." Certainly some god is being adored here. Is it the Christian one? One of my friends recently declared, "I've got a real commitment to this corporation. I've got responsibilities that touch the lives of many people. The well being of my family depends upon me and my job. The economy and the future of this community depend upon our company's success. My time is not my own." What god is he serving?

The goat heads and fruit offerings on the beach are very visible reminders of what goes on all over the world among all cultures. Most of us worship and give offerings to some god. We live in a world not of UNbelief but of many beliefs. Most often we believers contend not against atheism but against idolatry or false belief. When I see hardworking Brazilians forced to survive on less and less food so that someone else's profit margin can increase, I have no doubt they are being sacrificed on the altar of some god whose name is not Yahweh but Mammon. We Christians are called to resist these idols of death.

But we dare not so serenely reduce Joshua's words to a contrast between idols and the 'true' God. The choice he poses is between "the Lord our God" and "other gods." Our neighbors may be no less convinced than we are that they must battle the idols of death. But that is no guarantee that they follow and worship the same Lord God that we do. They certainly would not accept our characterization of their deity as a 'false god'. How will we react? Should we bear witness to our neighbors who are Buddhist, or Muslim or Hindu? If so, how? Should we grant them the right to witness to us?

Have you heard this argument: "Well, we all believe in the same God anyway, so it really makes little difference." Is this an accurate analysis? Would the Buddhists, Muslims and Hindus all agree that we worship the same God? Do we make that statement out of deep conviction and love for our neighbor, or out of an uneasy sense that we are facing a test for which we are not prepared? Do all people ultimately worship the same God? This is a true missionary question. Ever since Paul's sermon to the

Athenians about the 'unknown god' (Acts 17:16-34), Christian missionaries have grappled with that question. A myriad of answers have been given. Some answers appear more worthy than others when we examine them in the light of the Christ we seek to proclaim. Some answers have damaged and brought eventual shame to the missionary endeavor. What answers do we give to that missionary question now that the religious boundaries are no longer across the ocean but down the block and across the street?

This 'missionary question' is a mission and ministry question that all Christians must face it. When I scrutinize our mission and ministry in the United States from the overseas missionary perspective two helpful insights stand out.

1. We Christians do not now have, and never did have, a corner on the religious market. Not only did Jesus of Nazareth come into a world populated by many deities, the church was born and learned to walk in a society full of religions. Some of the first readers of the New Testament writings came to those writings with an understanding of God that was very different from the understanding held by the authors of those texts. Our creeds and doctrines were crafted over against other beliefs. Our ethic for living was forged in an environment teeming with alternatives. Historically, religious pluralism is not an aberration. It is the norm. It has a long history and has played a significant role in Christian formation. Instead of panic or protest, we should take up the challenges presented by today's pluralism.

Today's pluralism challenges us to find a way to witness boldly and faithfully without destroying others. We accept the global nature of life on this planet. Economically and ecologically we are all connected. Some Christians and non-Christians insist that this global reality coupled with current religious pluralism prohibits any group from proclaiming a universal truth. They point to the Crusades, the Inquisition and all of history's religious wars, and they argue that proclaiming a universal truth in our global reality can only lead to conflict and destruction. But I believe we must ask: is there a way to be a faithful disciple of Jesus Christ **without** proclaiming the universality of the Christ event? I don't think so. Is there a way for us to proclaim that universality without attacking or disparaging our neighbor and his/her religion? That is the task we face today.

I walked among the Brazilian people and their beach offerings as I walk among the neighbors and friends in the US: I walk as one convinced that the way of witness is the way of the cross. On this road we are not afraid to listen, love, and even die. This way of the cross redefines the success of the Christian witness. The successful witness is not the one that converts the most people. It is the witness that makes Christ and Christ's love most authentically and compellingly present.

2. Faithfulness to God is linked to fellowship in the community. I was pained when I learned that two members of my congregation were married in our church on a Friday evening and in the Umbanda community on Saturday. I reconsidered my reaction and realized that the Friday evening service had been done to honor the traditions of their parents and grandparents. The Saturday ceremony evidently expressed a commitment to their own community. Gods are worshipped and choices are made in community contexts. Faithfulness to God is sustained and defined within a fellowship of believers. It is, as the patriarch Joshua declared, "I and my household" who make the commitment to serve the Lord. Together we incarnate the hope and life called forth by our belief in God. The call to "choose this day whom you will serve" is always made to people embedded in a variety of communities.

How can your Christian community become a compelling, winsome fellowship? I don't have any magic formulas. I distrust those experts who claim to have seven easy steps to congregational success. Christian congregations can become life-sustaining and faith supporting fellowships only when they are faithful to Christ's Spirit who calls us to proclaim and incarnate hope in our world and to love and care for those whom God has placed in our midst.

Choose this day whom you shall serve. This day, and each and every day, you and I must decide which god we will serve. Whether we are running on sand amidst the offerings to other gods or are striding down the pavement of Main Street we are called to choose which lord will guide our lives and command our allegiances. As for me and my household, we shall serve the Lord.

17. HELMUT
(Hard lessons—the hard way)

I should never have opened the door. But I did and stepped into a year of frustration and guilt. It was 9PM on a cold, rainy night in southern Brazil. I was a few months into my eighteen-month stint as an interim pastor of a middle class congregation near downtown Esteio, just north of Porto Alegre. I opened the door and there stood a soggy, ragged, grizzled man. He had the look and the smell of a bedraggled street dog.

"G'evening pastor. My name is Helmut. I used to belong to this church." He extended a trembling hand and I reluctantly shook it. His face was gaunt and even in the dim light looked sickly. His clothes were some indeterminate color, between greasy gray and dirty brown. "Pastor, I wonder if I could sleep under the awning of the education center over there. It's pretty wet outside tonight." He sounded as if his vocal cords had been scrubbed with sandpaper. I strained to get past my repugnance at his appearance and odor. I wasn't sure that the conservative congregational leadership would approve of a homeless man sleeping on the premises. I wasn't so sure I wanted him anywhere near my wife and children either. But at this stage of my relationship to Helmut I believed that it was my duty as a pastor and my commitment as a Christian to respond.

"Man, I think it would be better if you were inside tonight. How about I get you a hotel room for the night?" When he rasped a grateful yes, I told him to go open the front gate while I got the car. I threw a blanket over the passenger's seat of my old VW and opened the car windows as Helmut shakily lowered himself into the front seat. Our city was not a destination for travelers. It had only two hotels. I parked the car, walked into the lobby and asked the young man at the desk, "Do you have a room available for tonight?"

The desk clerk answered, "Yeah sure" and reached for his registration pad. I waved to Helmut sitting in the car. When he walked through the door, the clerk looked up and snapped, "Not for him we don't. He can't stay here again." The same scene replayed, almost word for word at the second hotel. So, Helmut had a history and regrettably I had now become a part of it.

That night, and for the two nights that followed, Helmut slept under the awning of the education center. I felt that I should do more to help this wretch but didn't know where to begin. Then the rains stopped, the sun returned and Helmut was gone. I was relieved, and my guilt was assuaged. I didn't even bother mentioning the episode at that month's church council meeting.

Two weeks later, I was sitting in my home office on a sunny, brisk morning when someone knocked on the front door. My wife opened it and simply called, "Ron, this is for you." There stood Helmut. His hair was stiff with grease and dirt, his eyes bleary and red. He spoke gulping back tears.

"Pastor, I need your help." He looked down, shuffled his feet, then blurted out. "You can see I've got a drinking problem." Not only could I see it, I could smell it. Now he added a plaintive quiver to his rasp: "But pastor, I want to quit drinking, I really do. There's a detox program in the Porto Alegre Hospital. I need to have someone responsible to sign for me and commit me to the treatment. We could go to the clinic on the corner and the doctor can sign the papers. Would you do that for me, please?"

I naively leapt at his request. Here was a way I could truly help this poor soul. When we got to the clinic I was promptly disillusioned. The doctor pulled me aside. "Pastor, we've done this so many times before for this man. He enters the 8 week program and goes right back to drinking." I visualized the scrawny, shaky man sitting in the lobby who had fallen into my life. "But Dr. I can't just do nothing…" He looked over his glasses at me. I weakly added, "He has nowhere else to go." I believe the doctor understood my plight. With a sad grin and a shrug, he scrawled out his signature. "OK. For your sake pastor, I'll sign it." I came out of the office with the papers, threw the blanket back on the car seat and drove Helmut the twenty miles to the hospital. I drove home patting myself on the back, convinced that I had made a real difference in the life of this lost creature.

Eight weeks later the phone rang. "Pastor, I've finished the program, but I have no money to leave the city and nowhere to go." I felt a band tighten around my head as soon as I heard his voice. I was being drawn inexorably into Helmut's dark, eddying history. What else could I do? As I drove into Porto Alegre, my head began to pulse with pain. I drove up to the hospital entrance and there stood Helmut. At least his clothes were clean and he was freshly shaved. By now my headache had invaded the back of my neck. I fought off waves of nausea as Helmut yammered on and on.

"Well pastor, I've stopped drinking. I worked the program, yes I did. Went to all the meetings, put on some weight. Did you notice? Now, I've gotta get me a job so I can pay for a room. I'm a good mechanic, did you know that. Yes, plenty of experience. You wouldn't know of a place where I could stay for a few nights?"

I slowly shook my head. A hot poker of pain pierced my eyeballs. From the moment I'd heard his rasping voice on the phone, I'd known that this question was coming. I couldn't escape this woeful roller coaster. All my willpower was engaged in navigating the car home without vomiting. I surrendered with a weak groan. "I s'pose you can stay in the breezeway for a few days." We pulled into the church yard, I dug up a blanket for Helmut, gulped down some aspirin, and threw myself into bed and endured the first migraine headache of my life.

The next morning my head felt as though it had been pummeled by a heavyweight boxer. I shuffled into the kitchen desperate for coffee. My wife Lin was feeding the baby in his high chair. I filled my mug and slowly sat. I squinted against the sunlight that seemed to have tripled in intensity since yesterday. Lin gave me a sympathetic smile. "Do you feel as bad as you look?"

I tried to grin, "Actually, compared to yesterday, I feel better. What a hellish trip home! Say, have you seen—" She interrupted me. "Helmut? Yes. Gave him some toast and a cup of coffee about an hour ago."

I was afraid to ask. "What was he....how....um. What was your impression?"

Lin shrugged. "My impression? He was civil to me. Well spoken even. Thanked me and said he was going out to look for work. I told him he could use the back bathroom."

I sat and waited for the caffeine to slowly revive my brain. I tried to sort out my feelings about Helmut. My gut reaction was repulsion. Slam the door, hang up the phone, turn away. Snapping at the heels of that reaction was guilt. As a Christian pastor I'd relentlessly preached and taught that we Christians had been called by Christ to care for the lowest, the least and the lost. From the little I'd seen of Helmut, he epitomized all three categories. I wondered what sort of moral alchemy could transform my repulsion into genuine caring?

The church council was meeting that evening and I wanted to present the group with a strategy for helping one of God's lost sheep. I shared some ideas with Lin, she offered some suggestions and I went into the meeting with what I thought was a reasonable plan. I hadn't reckoned with Helmut's history.

I was always impatient at council meetings. The sessions at this new congregation were especially frustrating. Teobaldo, the president was a phlegmatic, dour man. He did nothing to speed along the proceedings and allowed everyone to chatter at once. I gritted my teeth as the group discussed the month's finances at a glacial pace. I squirmed in my seat as we repeatedly wandered into dead end discussions about what could be done if finances were better or why the young people weren't enthusiastic about worship. Finally the last item had been checked off of the night's agenda and Teobaldo asked, "is there any other new business?"

I cleared my throat, "Ahh, yes. Over the last few weeks I've been dealing with someone who says he used to belong to this congregation, his name is Helmut and—." A couple of the men snapped to attention and interrupted me.

"Helmut? You don't mean Helmut, that drunk?" Everyone began talking at once. I tried to reclaim their attention and stab their conscience at the same time.

"This man probably has a drinking problem but he's also one of God's children. Besides that, he's just come through a detox program and is trying to restart his life." Teobaldo's opinion wasn't altered, nor was his conscience moved. "Pastor, this guy's name is Helmut Steinbruck. We've known him forever. Some of us went through confirmation class with him. He had a decent profession, a wife and a couple of kids but ten years ago he started drinking and just went downhill. I'm telling you pastor, this guy is a hopeless drunk."

"Are you saying we should just turn our backs on him? Just let him kill himself drinking?"

"Pastor, I'm saying we'd be wasting our time. This is a guy who stole his daughter's hope chest to buy booze. One day his wife came home and the refrigerator was gone. Helmut sold it to buy liquor. His family won't have anything to do with him." Again, the conversations swirled about Helmut's many transgressions.

Their recounting of Helmut's history intensified my internal discord. My repulsion increased with each story, but at the same time my conviction grew that Helmut was truly the lowest, least and lost one that we needed to care for. I battled to preserve my own faith conviction.

I reminded the council of their Christian duty. I guilted them into a glum silence as I stubbornly presented by plan. Between the church and the parsonage stood a small storage shed. I would round up a used mattress and Helmut could sleep there. Our family would give him coffee in the morning and a dinner in the evening. He could use the bathroom facilities in the hallway. Once he got a job and had saved enough money to get an apartment he would leave. All of this was contingent upon Helmut staying sober. They didn't officially endorse my plan. They simply agreed to let me go ahead and try. I was on my own.

The next morning I explained the plan to Helmut. He was effusive. "Pastor, this is so great. You're a true man of God. I'll be working in no time. I won't make any trouble." I warned him that if he started drinking, he'd have to leave. "Oh no Pastor. I'm done drinking. I've learned my lesson. I'm going to stay sober." He helped me clean up the rickety storage shed. It had no windows, but it had a wooden floor. The door was crooked but the hinges still worked. We pushed the empty buckets against one wall and had enough room for the mattress that Jeni, the only woman on the council had donated.

Over the next two weeks we established a pattern. In the morning, we would set coffee and toast out on the patio for Helmut. Some mornings he'd already be awake and we'd chat as he smoked his cigarette and sipped his coffee. Other mornings we could hear him hacking and coughing in the shed but he'd stay inside until late morning.

He usually spent most of the day out in the city. He told us he was looking for work. In the evening, we would call him to come and get a plate of food. He'd usually take it to the shed. Later he would knock on the door, return the plate and then often go out for the evening. During those weeks, he and I would talk about the difficulty of finding work, the challenges of staying sober. His vocabulary and his speaking ability hinted at the intelligence of this broken man. My compassion for him deepened.

Then, one evening, when he returned his dinner plate, he asked me if he could borrow an umbrella. "I'm going to visit an old friend and it looks like rain. This cough won't clear up, especially if I get all wet." Since I'd heard him coughing into the night, and had begun to worry if he had some infectious disease I quickly handed over our umbrella. The next day when I asked for its return, Helmut looked down and stammered, "Pastor I'm really sorry, it's gone. I think I left it on the bus when I came home last night." Since I had lost my share of umbrellas too, I accepted his story.

A few days later, we sat together on the patio sharing our morning coffee. Sunny, my yellow parakeet, was cheerfully greeting the new day in her cage attached to the wall of the house. Helmut commented on her pretty singing. He asked her name then remarked, "Someday, I'd like to have a parakeet, when I get back on my feet. I suppose they're real expensive."

"Not so much. This one cost about fifteen reales." Inconsequential morning chatter, I supposed. But two days later, I came back from an afternoon meeting to find the birdcage empty. I stared up at the birdless cage and was both angry and ashamed: Angry at who had stolen my bird and ashamed that my first and only suspect was Helmut. I asked everyone, including Helmut if they knew what had happened. Of course no one knew anything.

Later that week, I was working on my son's bicycle and left a plier and screwdriver on the patio table. The next morning they were gone. The church lot was fenced in but the gate wasn't locked. Anyone could sneak into the churchyard and steal a few cheap tools. I didn't want to blame Helmut, my salvation project! But my suspicions would not die. I grew more dubious when I noticed that he was sleeping later and later in the mornings. He'd eat dinner in the evenings and hurry off into the night. I was always asleep when he returned.

Finally I decided to put my misgivings to the test. The door to the shack had a chain that Helmut hooked inside when he went to sleep. One night, after he left, I grabbed a padlock from the house and locked the chain. I hung the padlock key inside the back door. Sometime after midnight, I heard a pounding on the back door. As I padded through the darkness, I already knew. I flicked on the patio light, opened the door. Helmut swayed like a palm tree in the breeze. He didn't even need to speak. The smell alone told me the name of that old friend he'd been visiting these many evenings. I grimly handed him the key, and said, "Helmut, we'll talk in the morning."

I spent the night dreading the drama I'd face the next day. I mentally berated Helmut for his drinking, for his stealing and for humiliating me. I could only imagine what the council members would now say. Beneath my turgid thoughts, ran a river of guilt. I was going to give up on one of God's lost children. I had failed.

The morning was gray and damp. The theatrics I'd expected never materialized. I sat in the kitchen drinking coffee and listening to Helmut hack and cough in the shed. When I heard the shed door open I stepped out with his coffee. He shambled toward me, disheveled and bleary. He reached for the mug and his hands trembled. "Mornin' pastor."

I felt more sadness than anger. "Good morning, Helmut. I'm afraid this is your last cup of coffee here. We had a deal and you broke it. You were drunk last night. You're drinking again aren't you?" He cupped rough hands around the steaming mug, took a sip, and stared over my shoulder without a word.

"You're going to have to leave Helmut. Today. You can't stay here anymore."

He looked at me now, tears in his eyes. He jerkily nodded, set his coffee on the patio table and lurched back to the shed. I stood stunned by his silence. A minute later he emerged, a black plastic bag in one hand and an old coat in the other. Just as he reached the gate, he turned to me and rasped, "Thanks pastor." Three and a half months ago he'd shown up on my front porch, desperate and alone. Now he walked into the dreary morning mist and nothing had changed. I was relieved and I was ashamed that I was relieved. My mind believed I had done all that I could, but my heart still chided me for my failure.

Later that morning, I walked down the street to Jeni's home and glumly told her what had happened. She smiled sympathetically, "Pastor, don't be so hard on yourself. Lots of people have tried to help him. Sometimes, people like that have to hit bottom before they can change." I couldn't imagine how much lower Helmut could go. I asked her if she wanted her mattress back.

"No way. I think that man has tuberculosis. If I was you, Pastor I'd burn the mattress and the whole shed." I remembered Helmut's hacking laborious coughing and marveled at how I'd been able to ignore that possibility, how I'd even allowed him to be on the premises with my children playing in the yard. In the afternoon, I went over to the old shed. I pushed open the crooked door, took one step in and backed out gagging. Helmut had used the empty paint buckets as nighttime chamber pots. And despite having toilet facilities available, hadn't bothered to empty their contents. At least twenty reeking pots were lined up against the walls next to the mattress. No, I could not imagine any man falling any lower than Helmut had fallen. I emptied the buckets, lamenting the time and energy I'd wasted. I shamefacedly had to ask the council for permission to burn the shed. My little boys watched the flames with excitement. Within a few hours my misadventure with Helmut ended in a heap of gray ashes.

Several months later I was sitting in our living room on a warm spring evening. We had the doors and windows open hoping to catch some breeze. I heard heavy boots on the porch and jumped up to the door. A burly man in a uniform nearly filled the doorway. The mere sight of any official always reminded me of my status as a foreigner. Apprehension clamped my chest.

"Can I help you?"

"Good evening, sir. Are you the pastor?"

"Yeah, what's going on?"

"I'm from the São Leopoldo City Hospital. I've got a guy in the car who was a patient there but he's been discharged. He evidently has nowhere to go. He told us you'd give him a place to stay."

He stepped aside and I peered past him to the car on the curb. Sitting in the back seat staring at me, was Helmut. His pale face seemed to glow in the fading evening light. His eyes were dark holes in his face. I took a step back and put the bulky driver between me and that apparition in the car.

"No, no. He can't stay here. I've been through that once already. He has a family here in town. He does--a wife, some adult children. Let them take care of him."

"Sir, he told me they won't take him."

I took another step back and grabbed the door. "Well, I won't...I can't take him either. Sorry."

I closed the door, locked it, and peeked out the window as they drove away. My heart was pounding and my head throbbed. How long would my failure haunt me?

Warm spring slipped into hot humid summer. I was more than halfway through my stint as Esteio's interim pastor. I was enjoying the work with the youth and the choir. Other than dour Teobaldo, I'd come to appreciate the members of the church council. Jeni had become a dear friend. One day she came by with shocking news.

"Pastor, I just found out that Helmut is at a community house on the other side of town." I cringed at the mention of his name but was curious. "What's a community house?"

"It's a house that takes care of some who are sick or old. The owners take the people's disability payments or retirement benefits and use it to pay for room and board." I shook my head, chagrined. If I'd have known about such a place before... I hesitated. "So...did you hear how he's doing?"

Jeni answered, "No. The only thing I heard was that he couldn't walk."

A few days passed. Duty and curiosity overcame repulsion. I went to visit Helmut. The community house was a large residence with peeling yellow paint. I was greeted at the door by a short stout woman who simply pointed when I asked for Helmut. I walked in and saw beds everywhere. The place had the look and smell of a flophouse. Government benefits were always slim and no doubt barely covered the cost of food. Flies sluggishly buzzed in the oppressive heat. I finally found Helmut lying on a cot in a stifling back bedroom. His pajamas were clean, his color was better than I'd ever seen it. And he was sober.

"Hello Helmut."

"Hey, it's the pastor. Good to see you."

"I just found out you were here. Heard you can't get around. What happened?"

"Pastor, grab that chair over there. Sit down and I'll tell ya."

Helmut propped himself up on his elbows, grunted and slid himself into a sitting position, his legs stretched out in front of him on the mattress. "It all started when I was in São Leopoldo visiting an old friend. I stepped off the curb and I heard a crack and the next thing I knew I was lying in the gutter. My hip bone broke. Snap! Just like that. No reason whatsoever."

I shook my head in sympathy and could have told him that all of the booze he'd consumed in the past decade had turned his bones into brittle sticks. He hardly needed reminding.

"So, the ambulance takes me to the city hospital. You know, the one that's supposed to treat the poor. Pastor, I lay there for six days and they didn't do one thing for me." He stopped and tears began trickling down his ravaged cheeks.

"They...They wouldn't even come and help me get to the toilet and some days.... Some days, pastor, I lay there in my own shit for hours and hours. I was low pastor, low. I figured life couldn't get no worse."

He swiped a rough hand across his face. "But, I was wrong. One day the nurse comes in and says, 'you're discharged, you gotta leave.'

I says, 'leave? But I haven't even seen a doctor.'

She puts her hands on her fat hips and says, 'You're not a resident of this city, we're only obligated to keep you for six days and your time has run out. Your info card says you're from Esteio so that's where the driver will take you.'

They dropped me into a wheelchair, wheeled me to the hospital car and threw me into the back seat. The driver rolled in to Esteio and asked me where I wanted to go. I told him to go to your house."

I could still see that sallow, desperate face in the back seat of the hospital car. The guilt seared like acid in my belly. Helmut gave me a feeble smile.

"You said no. But you weren't the only one. Nobody...my wife, my kids, my old buddies...no one wanted anything to do with me. So the driver stops the car just before the bridge, the one that goes over the tracks and leads out of Esteio. He gets out of the car, comes around, opens my car door, scoops me up and plops me down on the grass. Then he drives away. I'm sprawled out there alongside the road, watching him drive away. I can't get to my feet, got nowhere to go, no one to care...That moment, pastor, right there, that was the worst, that was the lowest. I'd gone and wrecked my entire life, everything and everyone was gone. I laid myself down on the grass and figured I'd die right there."

The flies droned wearily in the stifling heat. Someone groaned in the next room. Helmut sat staring across the room. Even if I could have spoken, I wouldn't have known what to say.

"Then Sueli, the boss lady of this house, she happens to be crossing the bridge, sees me stretched out there on the grass. She comes over, I tell her I can't walk on account of my busted hip that by now has healed up all crooked. She offers to give me a bed and help me get my disability papers. So here I am, pastor." He smiled ruefully. "Still alive, but I sure as hell ain't kickin'."

I sat back in my creaking chair awash in a tumult of emotions: self reproach and guilt, but above all relief. Yes, I'd turned my back on him when he was desperate. I had failed him. But I couldn't bring myself to apologize. I would have been a hypocrite if I'd pretended I was sorry for what I'd done. Silently I rejoiced that I could leave this house and he could not follow me. I stood, grabbed Helmut's hand and murmured a prayer, thanking God that this poor soul had found a place of refuge and asking God to give him strength and healing. Then I escaped rejoicing back out into the sunshine and the dancing breeze.

I expected that Teobaldo and the rest of the leadership would ruefully smile at me and say, "We told you so." But to their credit they did not gloat over my misadventure. In fact, they helped secure a room for Helmut in a church run nursing home several miles out of town. Helmut lived out his years there. He continued to crave alcohol but since he was confined to a wheelchair, he never got to a store to buy a bottle. For the rest of his life he was sober.

My experience with Helmut sobered me up too. I soberly admitted that I was not a savior. I was reminded that my ability to care for and help another human being would always be limited by my own skills, by my commitments to my family and by my own sinful nature. Most importantly, I experienced in my own life, God's words spoken to Paul the apostle: ***"My grace is sufficient for you for power is made perfect in weakness." II Corinthians 12:9***

18. TOO LATE
(A Fiction)

"Oh, God, now what?" A sigh too deep for words escaped his lips. When the young pastor opened his front door and saw Clara silhouetted against the black Brazilian night he couldn't help himself. That groaning prayer didn't escape his lips but it did settle in his stomach. His heart, called to be compassionate and open, tightened in his chest and urged him to slam the door. Clara was trouble. No, Clara was trouble**some.**

A few weeks back she'd had a 'spell' in the back seat of his car. Every second and fourth Sunday the pastor and his wife would load the boys— a five year old and a three year old—and the baby girl, plus a guitar, a box of hymn books and a communion chalice into their VW bug and head south from the parsonage along the winding gravel road to lead worship at tiny little Arroyo Moreiera Church.

Some Sundays, as they wound around eucalyptus groves and down between rocky outcroppings, they'd encounter parishioners walking to worship. He was two years into this missionary call in a sprawling parish in southern Brazil. He'd learned early on that the pastor was expected to give a ride to whomever asked for it. No matter how crowded the car, he was expected to stop. Usually, an older person or two would squeeze in, take one of his children on his or her lap and they'd be on their way. Then, when he met the next group of walkers, and he'd stop, people would take a look at the stuffed bug and say, "thank you, we're fine" and he could head off to church, having fulfilled his pastoral duty.

But a couple of weeks ago they had an 'incident'. The already stuffed VW was groaning down the forest canopied curves to the church when Clara and her gangly thirteen year old daughter waved them down from the side of the road. He crunched to a stop in the loose gravel.

"Bom dia pastor. Obridago pela carona." Good morning pastor thanks for the ride. The pastor fought his irritation, tried to remember Jesus' words about the 'least of these.' Without even reconnoitering the back seat, Clara yanked the door open, and clambered into the narrow slot that already held three adults and two children.

From the back seat she now shrieked, "Celia, depressa!" Celia hurry up, get in here. She yanked her leggy daughter onto her lap. The VW, sagged a bit closer to the roadway, but gamely began rolling. Its willing engine was more Christian than the pastor. He felt like throwing the whole crew into the bushes and heading home for the day.

He had to down shift as they came to the last miles of the descent to the arroyo. Even with the windows open the air inside the bug was sticky with humidity and body heat.

Suddenly, Clara started gasping, "I think I'm having a heart attack!" She began chuffing shallowly.

"I've been having pains." She puffed like a steam engine. "I, I believe a devil is after me, trying to kill me!". Now her eyes began rolling white with panic. The pastor skidded to a stop, people started popping out of the car and he couldn't help but notice how they looked like those coiled snakes trapped inside of cans that clowns would open up at the circus to make the kids squeal. As the car emptied, Clara's breathing slowed. After a minute or two, she shook her head and smiled her snaggle-toothed smile.

"Whew. I...I... you know...its passed. I think I'm OK."

The pastor tried not to see her gap-toothed smile as an infuriating grin. He tried to remember the words from his old catechism. 'Speak well of your neighbor and put the most charitable construction on all that he (or in this case *she*) does.' He took a few deep breaths of his own and told himself, 'No, Clara simply had an attack of claustrophobia. She is a simple, poor soul. No, she did not do this on purpose.....'

Whatever Clara's motivation the journey proceded this way: The pastor got his family back into the car. His wife and baby daughter sat in the front. Clara and her daughter stayed in the back seat shared now only with the pastor's two little boys. The rest of the riders, perhaps knowing Clara better than he, were already walking the last mile to the church.

This was the Clara that met him as he opened his door. He had been looking forward to a quiet evening with his family. God knew he had too few of those. But, one look at Clara and he knew the chances of that happening were probably less than the chances of having snow in this subtropical village. So, he bowed to his destiny and asked her to come in.

"Pastor, pastor I'm sorry. Sorry to bother you so late but I don't know what to do..." She was clearly troubled and tugged at the sleeves of her dark blue hand-made sweater. The evening air was chilly. The Brazilian winter season was creeping in. Soon the winter rains would start. But tonight it was crisp and clear. Clara's clothes smelled of wood smoke from the cook stove at the heart of her kitchen and her work. That smoky smell was already imprinted in his mind as a marker of Brazil.

"Clara, calm down. What's going on?"

"This morning, I, we, Arnie and I ...we had a ... you know Arnie don't you?"

His mind clicked through the images of the hundreds of subsistence farmers he'd met over the years. Arnie didn't come to church, so he wasn't in that catalogue...But once, at a community churrasco, a Brazilian barbecue, he'd met him. Yes, he remembered: a tall, unkempt angular guy, with one eye slightly out of focus. Poor eating and poor hygiene had left him with only half his teeth. What he remembered most were Arnie's grin—half yellow, half dark gap—and his aura of raw-boned strength. He remembered thinking, 'Here's a guy who'd be a nasty drunk, one who'd break furniture and throw people through windows.'

"Yes, Clara, I do. What about Arnie?"

"Well, I wanted Celia to spend a few days with my mother in São Lourenço. You know my mother lives close to a school there and God knows the schools here are weak and there..."

He knew he should patiently listen but Clara could go on all night if he let her. He reached out for her hand.

"Clara, what about Arnie?"

She looked up now and tears filmed her dark eyes.

"Arnie... Arnie said she was too young to ride the bus and couldn't go and then Celia started crying and then Arnie got mad and threw a coffee cup at her and I told him he better not try that again and then he threw a plate at me and....and then I grabbed Celia and we locked ourselves in the bedroom."

The pastor could imagine that door, he'd seen his share of them in the houses of his parishioners--three rough sawn boards setting upright with a couple of strips of wood holding them together, two simple hinges and a primitive latch.

He could see Clara and Celia sitting on the sagging bed wrapped in each other's arms. He guessed Celia would be shivering and whimpering but Clara would be sitting, rocking a bit, waiting. He imagined this was not the first plate Arnie had thrown.

"Daddeee!" The pastor's four year old son came from out of his bedroom, scuffing the plastic toes of his footie pajamas against the hard wood floor and sliding into his arms. He was the cuddler of the family and when daddy was home he got as many hugs as he could.

"Good night hug Daddy."

"Ai querido! What a sweetheart!" Clara smiled wanly through her tears as the little guy leapt onto his dad's lap

The pastor looked at his mischievous son. His blue eyes were dancing with a secret joke. The scamp knew he was interrupting. He knew the household rules. But he was betting that his grin and squirming little body would get him what he wanted without too much resistance. The pastor wanted to tickle and laugh and roll on the floor with him, read another story to him and his brother. But here was Clara, needy Clara. Clara was his job, his assignment, his duty, his call.

"OK buddy, big hug. HMMMMM. Sleep tight."

He swatted the flannel bottom as the rascal scooted back to his bedroom.

"Sorry Clara. Go on. Arnie got angry and you went to the bedroom...Has Arnie ever hit you?"

Clara's gaze dropped to her red rough hands in her lap. The usual shrillness of her voice crumbled to a reluctant murmur.

"Never with his fists...."

With what then? he thought. Plates, cups, brooms, belts, shovels?...His grim reverie was brusquely interrupted by the memory of Clara gasping in the back seat of his VW. Her snaggle-toothed grin and the empty back seat. Tale of abuse or a variation on the victim theme that Clara seemed to play so well? Where on the continuum between cynicism and compassion should he settle? He mentally murmured his mantra, "Lord Jesus Christ, Son of God, have mercy on me a sinner!" and pushed his suspicions back down.

"OK Clara, OK. What happened next?"

"Well, Celia and I were sitting on the bed. It was quiet in the kitchen. Scary quiet. We could even hear the Buttow's calf bawling down the road. We just sat there. We waited. Celia was crying but I hugged her close to me. Crying seems to get Arnie even madder. Usually, pastor, usually I just let it go. I let him cool down and forget about it, then I pretend it didn't happen and he forgets about it and we keep, we keep....." her voice wavered.

"But I just couldn't do that Pastor. Not today. Celia was so scared and I got so, so damn mad...forgive me pastor."

He waved his hand as though brushing away a fly.

"We waited until we heard him go outside and hitch up the horses to go plowing. I said, 'Celia pack your clothes and don't forget your jacket. It gets cold along the lake in São Lourenço.' Then we caught the country bus and we got here at noon and at three o'clock Celia climbed on the direct line to São Lourenço, to my mother's. She's probably there by now."

She stopped talking and leaned back in her chair, relaxing in a way that announced: Here ends the story of Clara. He intuitively knew the next move in this oft played drama. It was HIS move. Where they went from here depended upon his creativity as well as hers. How this evening ended would be shaped by the depth of his compassion, the strength of his sense of duty and by the credibility of her need (or want).

He started slowly, with the obvious.

"So Clara...Celia left at three. Now it's eight and its dark and you're still here in town. No more country buses tonight. Why did you wait so long?"

She twisted her hands and they rasped like sandpaper.

"Usually, Arnie comes by afternoon into town with his tractor if I don't come home."

So. This was NOT the first time.

"But today, I waited and waited. He usually comes and we ...we neither of us say anything and we start over. But I don't know. Today he never came and now it's so dark and I don't know if something happened to him or if he's still mad or....."

"Clara, what do you want to do? What do you want ME to do?"

He never knew the best way to negotiate this moment. His own deep need to stay in control resisted such a risky question. His stomach ached even as he asked it. But his vocation, that life claiming call, the vulnerable Christ that he believed he was following, or maybe it was that heavier and seemingly simpler sense of duty...whatever it was, he had to ask the question and now resigned himself to accepting the answer.

"Pastor, could you take me home?"

He heard the he resignation in her voice. Over and over again he'd heard and seen variations of this theme in this country parish. He'd come to see it as a part of the national character: the sad but stoic acceptance of one's fate. He heard it in Clara's murmur.

Just as the woodsmoke had penetrated and forever bonded with her wool sweater, so this fatalism had been inextricably woven into her being. She would go back home because there was nowhere else for her to go. She would go back to Arnie because this was the life God had ordained for her. Only "se Deus quiser"...only if God willed it would her life change.

"OK Clara, can you wait for me out front. I'll get the car."

As he closed the front door he could hear his boys wrestling in the bedroom. His wife was changing the baby and the boys were rolling like monkeys on the bed.

"Hey guys, Mom will read your story tonight. Daddy's gotta take Clara home."

"Bye Dad," they giggled. His being gone was more normal than his being home. His cheeks puffed out in a self-pitying sigh. He looked over his wife's shoulder at their daughter, smiling up sleepily at them.

"Hon, I'll be back in about an hour." He kissed her neck and trudged out to the garage.

He and Clara clattered over the cobblestones out of town, then onto the dusty, serpentine road into the darkness of the countryside. His thoughts swirled with the dust behind the VW Bug.

How long, O Lord? How long can I stay in this parish?

Solidarity with the poor, he believed God was calling him to that. Here he was on a chill winter evening driving a beat up car on a dirt road taking a poor abused woman home. If this wasn't solidarity...

The gravel hitting the fenders underlay the stuffy silence in the car. He glanced over at Clara staring wearily into the dark. An old Peggy Lee song had been playing and replaying lately in his mind.... 'Is that all there is?' Is that all there is? Solidarity with Clara and Arnie and the thousands of others in his parish? What did it mean? He was ashamed, even afraid to admit it, but here it was: Solidarity with these poor Brazilian farmers might mean following Christ, he still believed that, but more and more he could see that above all solidarity meant being invisible to the world, just as invisible as they were.

He could spend his entire ministry here baptizing, marrying and burying, shortchanging his family, missing night time stories, and bedtime kisses and...nothing would change and no one would care and he would become more and more insignificant to the church and to the world. He was afraid of becoming a nobody. This was what shamed him the most. He and his family had been accepted and supported here. Even the skeptics, even the most suspicious parochial Germans, even they had come to appreciate them all and spoke well of him. But it was not enough. God had given him what he'd asked for and he was not satisfied. He felt like a selfish kid on Christmas morning. 'Is that all there is?' He was living with the humble ones; but... Carry the insignificance of the humble? How long could he carry that cross? If you are somebody who is loved by nobodies does that make you anybody?

"Here, pastor, turn here!" Too late Clara's words broke into his mulling. He hit the brakes, and slid to a stop in the middle of the road. The trailing dust cloud swept over them. He backed up, cramped the wheels hard and took the left hand turn onto an even narrower trail that followed the ridgeline. Shaggy barked eucalyptus trees lined both sides of the road like weary sentinels. They wound between boulders and finally started descending. About half way down the slope, Clara said, "just ahead pastor, you'll see a gate on the right." He slowed and stopped, Clara opened the crude gate, he coasted through, waited for her to clamber back in then they eased quietly over the faint track that led downward into the darkness.

Electricity replaced Clara's lethargy.

"You gotta cross the creek here pastor, but the bottom's hard. Not many cars come here but Arnie takes the tractor across all the time."

They forded the stream and started climbing. Clara shivered and murmured, "I just hope he's not drinking..."

An arctic chill of fear froze the pastor's hands on the steering wheel. Adrenaline surged through him. His weariness snapped into wariness.

"And if he's drinking...then what Clara?" Her silence scared him more than any words.

"Then what Clara?" He pressed the clutch to the floor and the car started coasting backward.

"No pastor, you gotta keep going or you'll lose traction."

He tried to hold down his frantic fear and keep his voice calm. "Clara, What if Arnie's been drinking, how is he?"

"Pastor, just keep going. Please. I'm sure... you never know with Arnie, sometimes he gets sad and cries, sobs even; sometimes he just sleeps, sometimes he...he can get real mean too pastor. But don't worry. I've seen it all before."

Now she pleaded in a voice as vulnerable as her daughter's. "Please, pastor, just get me home."

He started up the slope again, grinding in low gear since he'd lost all of his momentum. The faint grassy trail on the slope ahead was not much more than a silvery sheen under the headlights. Their feeble glow was no match for the deep blackness of the night. He could see no house lights up ahead. No surprise there. Even if they could have afforded them, electric lines didn't stretch out this far. If Arnie was home and if he was awake, he might only have a candle flickering on the kitchen table or a hissing gas lantern hanging from a hook on the wall.

Abruptly, the trail leveled out and grass gave way to gravel. To their left the hill sloped upward into the night. On the right, on the far edge of the headlight's reach, the low-slung silhouette of the house hugged the downward slope.

He coasted to a stop and cut the engine, but left the headlights on. The quiet was fearsome. Usually a pack of dogs broke into riotous barking whenever he'd enter a farmstead. No such greeting on this lonely hillside. The tick, tick, tick of the cooling engine was swallowed by the silence.

He'd been clutching the wheel and squinting into the night. Now he leaned back, looked across the seat to Clara and waited for her to push open the door. She sat immobile, hand frozen on the handle, staring at the shadowy door of her home.

She whispered, "I guess I—"

Suddenly and silently the door opened. Against the pale candlelight of the interior, the gangly hulking shadow of Arnie appeared. One hand clung to the doorframe. Was he steadying himself? He peered into the lights.

"Who's there?"

Clara opened the door and shouted, "Arnie, its me. Pastor brought me home."

It seemed as though it took all of Arnie's energy to grasp Clara's words. He slouched against the doorframe, slowly stretched his long neck to the sky then dropped his head, staring at his bare feet. Finally he lifted his face and slowly rasped, "And Celia? What about Celia?"

Clara grunted off the front seat and stood behind the sheltering vee of the car door.

"Arnie, let's just go inside." She stepped out from behind the car door and took a step toward the house.

Arnie loosened his grip on the doorframe and lurched forward.

He stood swaying in the gravel and growled, "Damn it where's Celia?"

Now the pastor jerked opened his door and jumped around to the front of the car. "Arnie, hey Arnie, good to see you again!"

Arnie's head and shoulders swiveled stiffly and his bleary gaze squinted into the headlights.

The pastor took another step forward and reached out his hands. "It's really chilly out here, Arnie, how about we go in for some coffee."

Arnie spoke with a surprising softness, as if he'd just noticed him. "Well, hello pastor...so you're here too."

Then without turning, Arnie stepped backward and appeared to be reaching back for the doorframe. His hand missed and he slipped into the dimness. The pastor took another step toward the humble cabin.

"No, Pastor, don't...."

Her curt words paralyzed him. Her voice, sharp now, and steely, slashed open his pastoral heart and with a rush, animal fear poured into his veins.

Blood pounded in his ears. A phrase throbbed in his mind. 'I am a stranger in an alien world.' How often he'd stiff-armed that thought aside as he charged into the routines of ministry in this place. But now, tottering on this little island of light in the middle of a great darkness, the reality of his dislocation locked him in its fierce embrace. 'I am a foreigner. This is not my place. What in God's name am I doing here?'

Arnie swiftly stepped out of the cabin's dusky dimness. For a moment he stood in the doorway, filling it with his gangly frame. Then he stepped forward and the pastor stopped breathing. Arnie now held a shotgun.

Clara screamed, but Arnie was deaf to her. He stepped toward the VW and the pastor's knees unlocked and for an instant he swayed. He caught himself and began sliding his feet backward in the gravel, keeping his eyes on Arnie. He abandoned all pretense of control and compassion. He whimpered, "now Arnie, Arnie.. Look I'm leaving now Arnie. I just brought Clara home I ...I didn't have anything to do with this......" Arnie matched steps with his backward shuffle. Now he was nearly even with the side of the VW.

Arnie's face was frozen in a lopsided grin as he raised the gun. For an instant, the young pastor dared believe that just maybe this was all some stupid old farmer joke.

The thunder of the blast and the burning pain met in the middle of his chest. As he spun and fell, the image of Arnie's half empty, stupid smile hovering above the barrel of the shotgun burned on his retina. He lay on his side near the front wheel of his old car. He did not move. His first thought was, 'who will do Sunday's worship services?' He released that worry with relief. As the chill of death set him trembling he wondered if he'd be buried under the pine trees in the lonely cemetery beside the church. So far from home. The blood pulsed slower and slower down his chest onto the gravel. He could feel his wife's warm neck beneath his lips and he could see his baby girl's dark eyes smiling, smiling up at him and hear his boys' joyful laughter. He would have cried but it was too late for tears.

19. GOING HOME
(A fiction)

John sat in the kitchen beside the wood-burning stove. The only blessing in this rain was its variety: The rain pattered, drizzled, misted, or pounded day after day. The air was so full of cold winter rain that the inside walls were wet to the touch. John sat in the kitchen beside the crackling wood stove and was silent. He'd been silent now for three days. Susan had tried to reach him that first day. She'd prodded him out of bed that Monday morning. "Hey, guy, its your day off. Going to sleep it away?" He lay under the comforter, his red hair a nimbus on his pillow. His eyes seemed unable to settle on her. They were caught by some distant universe. He'd slowly eased out of bed that first day, drank the traditional gaucho green tea that she'd prepared. But as that first gray rainy day of silence ended, more and more of him was absent. She'd led him to bed, tucked him in after putting their three little ones down for the night. "Daddy's not feeling well, just leave him alone." That explanation easily satisfied them. He was so often gone that his absence did not feel strange at all. It was easy to ignore him.

Now as this silence moved in to the third day, she felt that John, all of him, except for this lanky shell of a body, the beard and the halo of hair, all of him had left for some distant universe. What propellant had carried him so far, so far away from her and from here? Was it hate? Fear? Anger? Was it pain that had launched him into this silent world? What was it like there she wondered? No shouting, she supposed. Certainly no nagging from her about helping at home, being gone so much, and what were they doing anyway in this bleak corner of southern Brazil. No demands from the church council that he do more visitation, that he spend less parish money, that he keep better track of expenses, or that he be more accessible to parishioners. He sat wrapped in a blanket on the stool beside the stove with his strong back curled like the drooping fronds outside. His eyes focused beyond the rain weeping window, beyond the slick cobblestone courtyard, beyond the gray, stolid walls of the Lutheran church where in four days he was supposed to climb the creaking steps in his black robe and once more preach the Good News to his flock. His eyes focused somewhere, but not anywhere that Susan could see.

Susan wondered what to do next. He'd had his moments before--hours, even a day once last year when he'd simply gone away for awhile, taken a side road into a passive silence. He would be conscious, eyes open, could move about but he would not respond to questions or demands. He would simply look through you and turn away. He'd always come back before, slowly, wearily, as if he'd been on some exhausting journey. He'd reluctantly return to his office to write a sermon or bend himself into the battered parish car to visit some family in crisis.

But as the misty drizzle slowly extinguished the gray light of this third day she knew that tomorrow she'd have to act. Maybe she'd talk to the parish president. She cringed at the thought. He owned the town's largest feed store and he'd been openly suspicious of a foreigner for a pastor. He was a cynical, husky Teutonic Brazilian who smelled weakness the way a dog smelled fear. She suspected he'd react with the same sort of savage glee. Certainly she'd have to call the missionary president in São Paulo. Maybe even a phone call to the US. Either way she'd have to get to the phone center downtown, wait for a booth to be available, give the number to the operator, enter the booth and wait for the ring. The connections were always bad, the booths weren't soundproof and you always prayed that the party next door wouldn't be too deaf and shout at the top of his lungs or that it would be one of the town's many gossips, salivating over your scandalous news. There was no such thing as a casual phone call in Brazil. She'd need a baby sitter for the kids, and now for John too. God help her. What was she going to say? " My husband has fallen in to a catatonic state and I can't reach him?" "John is having some personal problems and we need to get out of here?" My God, what the hell are we going to do?

How sadly ironic. Just in the last few months she'd gotten over her aversion to this town set on the edge of the range and farm land that stretched westward for hundreds of miles. She'd finally found some friends at church, the kids loved playing in the yards of the neighbors and she'd learned enough of the language to laugh and gossip with the other moms. That first year had been achingly painful for her. John had exuberantly charged into parish life. His flaming red hair and deep laugh had filled every room and he'd zipped eagerly to every corner of his vast parish.

Like a threatened mother hen, she'd held back, felt threatened and protective of the kids. She was not by nature a shy person, but she felt herself shrinking. During that first year their joint resolve to embark on this adventure had seemed more like John's call to ministry and her cross to bear. But as year one passed, somewhere in the universe of their life together, a pendulum began a subtle swing.

As she rediscovered her voice, her passions, and her joy, John began to move in the other direction. The facts were what they'd always been. He was a pastor to seven hundred families scattered over a three hundred square mile area. His boyish jauntiness and energy had allowed him for a time to ignore other critical facts. They expected him to run the parish as it had always been run. They expected him to be an administrator. They expected him to listen to the demands of the elders. These gritty truths mercilessly scoured and pitted his shiny self-image day after day.

So, the ironic pendulum of their life had swung. That much Susan knew. But she could not grasp how that swing had managed to paralyze this laughing, lovable man, how it could turn him into an old, cold mute, rocking on the stool by the now cooling kitchen cook stove. What nerve had been torn, what old wound ripped open by all of this? She couldn't see through the mist in her own mind. She couldn't figure out the equation, the A + B =C of his withdrawal. First, she'd been concerned, then angry, then afraid. Now she felt the first spasms of panic squeezing across her chest.

The dark came early and the rain continued its dismal dripping. By seven thirty she'd read stories and gotten the kids ready for bed. She made them go kiss their daddy good night. They were only a little sad. After all Daddy didn't seem all that sick. But they were shy as they went into the semi-dark kitchen. The plastic bottoms on the feet of their pajamas scuffled on the tile floor. One by one they came around in front of him and kissed his check above his burnished beard. "Night Daddy," they murmured and skittered back to their room. Susan stood in the doorway watching. Did he tilt his head a bit there? He did nod a little nod. Surely he did. She could hear the kids giggling and bouncing on the bed.

The rain was falling harder again, a sullen steady streaming against the kitchen window. She moved to him then and the tears rolled down her cheeks. She knelt in front of him, hands gripping his shoulders, "John, please. Come back. Please. I can't do this alone. We don't have to stay here. Please let me help. I can't go where you are John. I can't go with you. You have to come back." She tried not to sob, and her knees ached from the hard damp tiles. She thought she saw flicker in his eyes, like a camera refocusing from far to near. But the moment passed and nothing happened. Just the rain against the black panes, just the monotonous dripping from the eaves. She felt decades older as she struggled to her feet. She put one hand beneath his arm and pulled and he followed her, slowly, meekly into their bedroom. He took two steps and rolled into bed, pulled up the covers and turned toward the wall and was asleep.

The kids had spent too much time trapped inside and were electric. She finally got them settled down and sleeping. Then she sat down at the dining room table with the phone directory and the address book and made a list of all of the numbers she'd have to call tomorrow. She even included the number of the hospital in the city, though she hoped no one would suggest they go to that dank, gray place reeking of desperation. Whatever it was that had driven John so far away from himself would not be discovered in that place, nor would it be found anywhere in this land. The catalyst may have been here, in this parish, in this place and its demands. But the fuel it ignited lay inside of him, within his history.

Her eyes burned with weariness. She put away the books and turned out the lights. She walked across the room and the page with tomorrow's phone numbers lay ghostly white upon the dark wood of the table. She brushed her teeth in the chill damp bathroom, then quickly shed her clothes and pulled on her flannel gown and sank into bed. Tomorrow, O God what will be tomorrow? She held on to that prayer as she tumbled into sleep.

Her eyes snapped open. What was it? The silence? Yes. The rain had stopped. Not even any dripping from the eaves. But something else had summoned her from deep sleep. Then she felt his hand stroking her hair, weak and feeble, the hand of a convalescent. She hardly dared roll over. Slowly she twisted from her side to her back to her side and yanked her night gown straight. At last she dared to look into face. He returned her look. His eyes overflowed with tears, and they trickled down into his beard. Over and over again he whispered, "I'm sorry, I'm sorry." She pulled his head to her breast and her tears mingled with his. Tomorrow they'd start the journey home.

20. GOD LIVES UP THERE!
(A fiction)

Three children sat on a log beside the stream. The three of them had spent most of the long summer days together. By some happy coincidence, all three lived on the same block and by an even more amazing spin of fortune's wheel all three households had not enrolled their kids in the endless classes, camps, and outings that regimented and consumed the rest of the neighborhood children's days. These three had spent the summer learning one of life's greatest lessons: how to entertain themselves.

Stacy, the only girl, sat in the middle. She wore glasses designed to coax her lazy eye into action. No one ever accused any other part of Stacy of laziness. She needed no national health promotion to get her outside for an hour a day. She, Ben and TJ had just run from the park swings, across the picnic grounds and now were catching their breath alongside Nelson Creek.

Stacy turned her clear face to the sun bleached sky dotted with thin soap foam clouds. She pointed up and dramatically announced. "God lives up there."

Ben tipped his Twins cap back and squinted into the blue. "I don't see nuthin."

"Duh, God's invisible, Everybody knows that." Stacy spoke with the serious, unflappable conviction of an eight year old.

TJ hopped up on the log and extended his arms, pretending he was a high wire artist. He was a year older than Stacy, but shorter than her and stockier.

"My Mom says God is everywhere. How can he be in the sky and be everywhere too?" He looked down at Stacy who still sat in the middle of the log. He expected a sharp reply or even a whack on his shins. But she looked up at him, wriggled her shoulders and then turned back to the sky.

Ben appeared to be ignoring the conversation. He was a few months younger than Stacy but something in his thin face, the eyes maybe, made him seem older. He pretended to fall off of the log, then sat on his butt and slid down the bank and began looking for flat rocks to skip. He held up a smooth cookie-shaped sandy stone for his friends to see before he side armed it across the water. It hit once, twice, then hopped up to the opposite bank. He stooped to look for another rock and spoke into the sandy shore.

"My Dad talks about God a lot. He says 'God damn this car.' 'God damn this job.'" Benny stood up and flipped another rock, then turned to his two friends. "Last night when I spilled my milk he even said, 'Goddamn it Benny, be more careful.'"

TJ joined Ben along the stream. Stacy straddled the log. With pontifical certainty she declared, "Your daddy is cussin' and that's a big mongo sin and he's probly gonna end up in hell."

Ben shrugged his shoulders and flipped another stone. But TJ glared up at Stacy on her log, "Oh yeah? Well, Stace—if you know so much, where's hell?"

She swung her leg over the log and stood up, stared at the two boys and started to pound her foot on the grass.

"Down! Hell is down. Everyone knows it's down deep in the ground and its hot and smelly and the devil lives there."

Ben turned to Stacy with the glimmer of a grin. "Wouldn't bother me if my dad went there." He was trying to lighten the mood, an unconscious strategy that even some eight year olds are forced to learn.

But something in Stacy's steely answers rankled TJ. Her unusual seriousness confused and irked him.

"You don't know nuthin'. Last night on Discovery Channel they had a whole show on the inside of the earth. There's no place to live deep under the ground. Its all hot lava and gunk, like what comes out of volcanoes. Nobody could live there, its boiling. I think you're just makin' it up to make Ben feel bad."

To their total shock, Stacy turned and started running through the woods. Like adults, children run for all sorts of reasons. Sometimes they run for the sheer joy of motion, the joy of momentarily defying gravity and slicing through the air. Like adults they run as a way of saying 'yes!' to life. And sometimes, like adults, children run because they are afraid. Adults have many different methods of fearful running. They immerse themselves in work, or they turn to drugs or they have affairs. But children have fewer options.

So Stacy ran weaving through the trees until she found the park trail, then pounded along the gravel until her lungs burned in her chest and her legs felt like lead pipes. She leaned against the monkey bars in the playground gasping and gulping for air. TJ and Ben came trotting up as her heart slowed its pounding.

"Hey, crazy girl, what the--" TJ began. He choked off his words when he saw, of all things, tears trickling down Stacy's cheeks. Neither of the boys had ever seen Stacy cry. They stood before their friend in reverential silence. She was not sobbing, yet those clearly were tears dribbling down her dusty red cheeks and she made no effort to wipe them away. Stacy leaned back against the monkey bars ladder. She gazed past them out toward the swings that hung slack and empty, and then she swept the back of her arm under her nose.

"Ben, I'm sorry I said those bad things about your dad."

Ben moved close and put his hand on her sweaty arm. "Geez, Stace, geez, don't feel so bad. My daddy is kinda mean and I've thought worse things about him."

Stacy shifted her eyes, slowly, painfully to meet his. "Benny, its MY dad, he's... he's gonna die." She spoke with a fierce sadness that chilled the boys. But they were friends and didn't retreat.

TJ edged in and stood beside her and asked, "But how do you know?"

Now Stacy started gasping back the sobs. "Last night we had a family meeting and daddy told us he has something bad, real bad that's making him sick; something called pancratic cancer and that the doctors couldn't do nothing to help him get better."

Like adults, children don't always know what to say in the face of another's great pain. But children know what friendship is and what friends are for. Ben and TJ hugged their friend and TJ murmured as they hugged, "When your daddy dies he's gonna go up to heaven and he'll be with God forever."

And then, all together, they cried.

21. LIVING AND DYING
(Remembering Funerals)

A couple of Saturdays ago I sat in our worship center listening to our choir director and resident internationally renowned concert pianist playing a work by Chopin. I had my eyes closed and let this beautiful classical music transport me to celestial heights. Then, as she had warned us beforehand, the third movement began with its very familiar funeral march. DaDaDaDummmm, DaDaDaDummmm.... My thoughts stopped rising on the musical updrafts and plummeted earthward. I began to remember funerals—funerals I'd attended, funerals at which I'd officiated, funerals painfully and indelibly incised into my memory.

Grandpa Rudolf Heupel, died in 1960 at 67, cause of death: cerebral hemorrhage while sitting in a restaurant in the resort town of Detroit Lakes, Minnesota.

I have only one image left from the funeral. I was only eleven years old and the only grandchild allowed to attend this traumatic event. I was deemed 'old enough'. How old is old enough to face death? Here is my one memory fragment: We are standing in the country church where Grandpa had served as pastor for twenty years. It's only a couple of miles north of my home, set on a hill, overlooking the Dakota prairie. The building had closed a year or two earlier when the congregation merged with Immanuel Lutheran in town. But this unexpected funeral for Pastor Rudolf could only have been held in one place: Trinity Evangelical Church, more popularly known as the Heupel church. Grandpa Rudolf had not only been pastor during the church's golden era, he'd also been a bone setter, a dispenser of pills, a chiropractor, masseuse and, according to the thousands of people who'd visited him over the years, a healer. The church is packed with sturdy, German-Russian bodies. Shoulders thickened by farm work are pinched by seldom worn suits. Sniffles compete with swallowed sobs to fill the high ceilinged room. The doors stand wide open, flat against the outside walls. The windows have all been thrown up as high as they go. People stand three deep outside the church. The only words I remember from that day were spoken by my aunt Helen. As we cluster beside the open coffin, she murmurs, "He looks just like he always looked when he'd nap on the sofa, lying on his back, hands folded across this chest."

More than five decades later, those words and that image flicker across my mental screen, especially when I tip back my lazy boy chair, fold my hands across my chest and take my afternoon nap.

Joel Elmo Anderson, died 1977 at 19. Cause of death: hit by a car in Arizona as he unheedingly stepped out into the street.

I came to Peace Lutheran Church in Fargo in 1976. Joel was the president of the youth group when I arrived. He was also the firstborn son of the senior pastor. He was restlessly looking for direction in life. I remember him lying in his coffin, his long blond hair tied back with a red bandanna. One of his buddies had laid his harmonica on his chest. He had a bit of that enigmatic smile he always carried. A young man searching for his way through life was blindsided by death. Thankfully, the bishop conducted the service. Joel died in winter and as the coffin was carried out of the back of the church and put into the hearse, the wind knifed through all of us and snow swirled and eddied into the building. The congregation was singing **Children of the Heavenly Father**...."though he giveth or he taketh God his children ne'er forsaketh...." I stood with the family in the narthex. We watched his young friends recruited as pall bearers carry his coffin out. I still can hear his mother softly weeping, and murmuring. "Poor Joel he will be so cold, so cold." I cannot sing that song without thinking of Joel and of his family wracked by sadness and grief. We hardly ever ponder how short life can be.

Brazilian parishioner, name forgotten, died in 1982, age forgotten, cause of death forgotten.

I started work in my first Brazilian parish in May of 1982 after seven months of language training. Morro Redondo was a farming community in southern Brazil, inhabited ironically by people of the same Germanic stock as my hometown in North Dakota. With over three thousand people in the parish, it was not surprising that one of my first official acts was a funeral. Brazilian law insisted that burial had to be within twenty four hours of death. That was scarcely enough time for a fledgling speaker to prepare a funeral message. But I somehow managed to get some pages written and I had the official order of service book from the national church so I hoped I'd survive the event.

In small communities, funerals are social events. Advent Lutheran Church was packed with family, friends, and neighbors—all who took seriously Paul's words that we need to rejoice with those who rejoice and weep with those who weep. I do not remember what I said, but I remember sweating beneath my black robe and following the coffin down the aisle, and out onto the sun baked afternoon.

The cemetery was an eighth of a mile from the church and the entire congregation followed the coffin down the graveled main street. Men from the community took turns spelling the official pallbearers as we quietly moved toward the cemetery. No one spoke, only the crunch of gravel filled the warm afternoon.

I remember walking under the old stone portal that led into the cemetery and walking under a row of tall eucalyptus trees along the side of the fence. When we came to the gravesite, the men set the coffin on boards laid across the opening. I took up my position at the head of the coffin and the entire congregation gathered around me. I read the burial service as I found it in my service book, watched along with everyone else as the men lowered the coffin and filled the hole with dirt. I pronounced the final blessing and closed the book with glad relief. But when I looked up the entire crowd was staring at me with what seemed like expectation. A chill panic pierced my hot robes. What did they want? What had I forgotten? I frantically opened up the service book and scanned the funeral service again. No, I had clearly followed the official liturgy from beginning to end. Yet it was quite clear that for these people, this congregation, there was some unfinished business. As the silence stretched on, I could hear the beginning of anxious murmurings. How could I be a pastor to these people if I didn't know how to tend them in the dark times?

Francisco Neumann, wizened patriarch of the Morro Redondo Neumann clan, discerned my plight. Most of these farm families were long accustomed to educated pastors coming into their humble community and telling them how to believe like Christians, how to behave like Christians, how to marry, baptize and bury. None of them dreamt of instructing a pastor. But Francisco with his compassion and his gray haired wisdom read the panic in my face and slipped quietly beside me. "Pastor, you have to tell the people that they now can place their flowers on the grave." My voiced quavered as I invited the congregation to come forward and place their flowers on the pile of dirt. Francisco tugged on my gown again, "Now, Pastor, on behalf of the family thank them for coming and tell them to go in peace." I repeated his words. It was as though everyone had been released from a magic spell. The tension broke. Quiet conversations and even soft laughter broke out as people started walking slowly out of the sun back under the shade of the trees on their way home.

I walked back to the parsonage. My gown was drenched with anxious sweat. I had survived and I had learned a valuable lesson. We pastors come into congregations with knowledge, insights and some wisdom. But we cannot become the pastor the congregation needs unless we are willing to listen and learn from the people. They are the ones who carry the traditions, the practices, the hopes and the fears that are not found in official books. The congregation helps to shape us into the pastors we need to be.

Elmer Roland Baesler, died July 31st, 1992 at 67. Cause of death: brain tumor.

I spoke at my own dad's funeral. Somehow saying things out loud in front of people is what makes them real for me. I remember talking about my dad's great, loud, booming voice. He could shout above the noise of machinery. When he stood up on his grain harvester and shouted for me to bring the grain truck, even if he was half a mile away, I could hear his call floating through the dusty air. He had a clear, enthusiastic tenor voice and could sing the old hymns with a joy that rattled the windows. But over the years the cancer had taken away his joyful singing, his strong shouting, his gleeful joke telling. Cancer had stripped him of his voice. He fell silent. Yet, through the years I still heard him speaking to me of integrity, the importance of doing a good job, the value of honesty. I had his voice inside of me. But on the day of his funeral I announced to family and friends that somewhere I was sure he was singing again and telling stories. Somewhere his voice was once again ringing loud and clear.

We buried Dad in the same cemetery that held his father-in-law Grandpa Rudolf, his dad and mom, his brother killed in World War II and Mitchell, his firstborn son who died after only three days of life. Just beyond the trees, the steeple of Trinity Evangelical Church cut into the painfully blue sky. The August day was warm, the meadowlarks sat on the metal fence posts around the cemetery and never stopped singing. All around the cemetery, the wheat fields ripened, turning slowly from green to gold under the hot sun. If the hail stayed away, the harvest would be decent.

Larry Glen Baesler, died September 9th, 2009, Cause of death: cancer

My only brother, younger by two years. We had slept in the same bed growing up. We had roomed together in college. Gregarious, extroverted and passionate about nature, a reverse image of his older introverted, inward looking brother. Riddled with cancer and dead at fifty seven.

My memories of the time we spent at his funeral in Rapid City, South Dakota are all seen through a window smeared with tears and sorrow.
We had a gathering at the Lutheran Church on the night before the funeral. Colleagues told stories of Larry's hunting and fishing exploits, his profound gift for savoring life and his willingness to serve others.
I was his only brother. I had a unique perspective. I am a man trained to speak before crowds. I stood and I spoke but the words tasted ashy in my mouth. What I said didn't come from my heart. All my heart words had been dissolved by salty tears and acidic regrets. I felt as though everyone there knew him better than I did, loved him better than I had.

I sat beside mom hunched in her wheel chair. She had the look of a bewildered animal stunned by a blow to the head. I swallowed a groan. How absolutely unfair that she should have to bury her son—the one who could always make her laugh, who would even dare to pick her up and hug her, who had been her rock during the treacherous, sorrowful journey that ended with dad's death. Bereft, we all were bereft. Larry's son spoke, Pastor Chris, a strong man and a suffering son. Larry's son-in-law Matt spoke and of all of us, his grief was most clearly seen. Larry had been the sort of dad that his real dad hadn't been. To find that man in your life and have him for only a few years, was a blow that sent this strong Marine reeling.

Next day was the funeral. All I have from that day are disconnected memories, snips of images cut from that blurry film of that afternoon. Though we'd known for months that this moment was coming, I'd been half a continent away. Even though I'd officiated at innumerable funerals and even preached at my own father's funeral, the brutal reality of this day staggered me. I saw the simple wooden box, not much larger than a shoebox, sitting on the altar. My brother's ashes. All of his playfulness and passion, his slick open field running and silly humor, his insights and intelligence, all of his love and labor reduced to handfuls of ashes.

I joined others in the family who laid their hands on the box. I said a prayer but it was stillborn on my lips. I choked along as the congregation sang **Children of the Heavenly Father**.... "Neither life nor death shall ever, from the Lord his children sever, unto them his grace he showeth, and their sorrows all he knoweth." I had no strength to believe that. Sorrow sapped my strength to hold on to God's promises. I rode the current of the congregations's faith, allowed the ancient stream to carry me on.

I think that is why we have funerals, why human beings everywhere gather in some fashion to recognize the death of a loved one. We the living gather to remind each other that life and love have not been obliterated. We gather to hold each other up, to carry each other forward. We gather because we need each other to live.

22. BIRDS FOR THE WORDS
(Thinking about weddings)

Once upon a time weddings were a matter of words. Of course there was the gown, the procession down the aisle, flower girls who, depending upon their ages and disposition, would or wouldn't scatter flower petals on the aisle. All of these things were meant to be a beautiful framing for the central moment that involved words. The religious leader of the day said most of the words. He even said the vows that the couple nervously repeated. Sometimes the smiling couple opted for the even simpler 'I do' and the ceremony was complete. But today things are different. In our post-modern or post-post-modern culture people trust less and less in the power of words. Contemporary culture has once again fallen in love with the visual, and with multi-sensory events. We who conduct wedding ceremonies are seeing all sorts of new symbolic and visual 'proclamations'. These events are meant to communicate or punctuate some aspect of this newly established marriage.

Now when these actions involve inanimate objects, the results are fairly safe and predictable. The unity candle ceremony is simple and obvious enough. Before the ceremony begins, the mothers of the bride and the groom, representing the two birth families, come to the altar. Each one lights a candle that flanks the unity candle in the center of the altar. Later in the ceremony, the bride and groom use those two candles to light the unity candle. Out of two families has come a new family, yet each person retains their identity. Simple, straightforward, and safe. Unless the nervous bride, after taking out her candle to light the unity candle fails to secure the candle in its holder and it falls onto the altar setting the paraments on fire.

I've seen vials of multi-colored sand poured into one container to symbolize unity, glasses of red and white wine poured together into a single chalice. All of these are attempts to express what the words have already declared: the two shall become one and what the Lord has joined let no man (or woman) put asunder.

The newest and most dramatic symbolic additions to marriage services are the introduction of living creatures. What better way to express the joy, unity, and heart lifting spirit of the day than by incorporating some living being into your service? Of course you have to assume the risks involved. If you have invested your heart (not to mention your money) into the symbolic statement these creatures will make, then you will have to live with whatever happens and allow the symbol to speak. And lest we forget, animals are less predictable and containable than words.

One couple handed out small butterfly shaped boxes to all the guests. These boxes contained, you guessed it, living butterflies. After the ceremony, the guests were invited to stand outside the church, and open their boxes. The joy and the delight of the day would be symbolized by the flickers and flashes of color rising into the sky. The guests gathered, the couple stood dramatically in the church doorway, and the boxes were snapped open. A moment of silence than a buzz, then nervous laughter. In every box lay a multi-colored, archly sculpted dead butterfly. Here and there a wing fluttered once or twice in one of the boxes but mostly they were all dead. So how seriously were we all to take the symbolic action? Was this a still-born marriage? Or merely a bad batch of butterflies?

Another couple bought the same symbolic butterfly action package. (Who markets these things anyway?) They hadn't counted on the temperature dropping on the day of their wedding. By the time of the ceremonial box opening, the poor little creatures were too cold and stiff to fly, they lay shivering in their boxes. The guests carefully took the fragile insects out and set them on the bushes around the church door. Now, what did _that_ symbolic action mean? Was this to be a handle-with-care marriage? Was this an omen of a fragile, frigid marriage?

The best events, from a spectator standpoint, involve birds. Of the many "birds at wedding stories," that I've heard and participated in, here's the best. The ceremony is in a hotel ballroom that looks out over the ocean. Seated in the ballroom you can only see the ocean. But if you go to the balcony, you can see the paddleball courts directly below, the sandy beach, and then the ocean.

The bride and groom, or maybe a clever marketer, have devised an event freighted with meaning. Of course it involves birds--doves to be exact. Such beautiful, gentle, sleek creatures. Neither bride nor groom has ever really gotten very close to a dove, but in the pictures as interpreted by the salesperson, they are the perfect symbol. A cage with half a dozen doves stands near the balcony during the ceremony. The noise from six cooing, squawking doves is accompanied by the burbling of the champagne fountain that has been set up behind the chairs. This guarantees that the audience catches significantly less than half of the pastor's words. How appropriate then that this bride and groom have chosen a vivid symbolic action to announce the wonder of their union.

The vows have been spoken and the rings exchanged. Now, hand in hand, the couple moves slowly to the cage. The groom reaches in and desperately grabs one of the frantic birds. He finally secures it with both hands. He allows his serious scowl to relax as he makes his capture. He even risks a smile as he half turns to the congregation. Just as they have scripted, he elevates the bird (as a priest would elevate the host) and he proclaims, "may our marriage have joy!"

He tosses the bird up and out over the balcony rail. There is a blur of white, the dove frantically scrambles for altitude, then slowly sinks below the sight line of the congregation. The bride and groom peer over the railing. The bird does a steep, barely controlled glide onto the paddleball courts.

This eager bride and groom have rented a cage full of doves with clipped wings! And they are novices in the ways of birds. They have invested money in this dramatic moment. They have invested meaning into this symbolic event. By God, these birds were hired to proclaim and proclaim they will! Maybe that first bird suffered from the national disease of obesity. The bride grimly clutches after another hapless dove. She turns to the congregation, elevates her squirming captive: "May our marriage have unity!" She pitches the bird as far as her gauzy gown will allow. Sadly it follows the trajectory of its comrade. A desperate scramble for altitude, then an arching plummet to the paddleball courts below.

An experienced preacher knows when to cut the message short. If the bride or groom begins to pale, or to wobble in front of the altar the pastor skips a few paragraphs and cuts to the chase. But this moment is the couple's first experience at 'proclamation'. They charge stubbornly ahead: "May our marriage have beauty!" "May our marriage have delight!" Every verbal proclamation is followed by a visual proclamation of desperation and defeat. Two birds are left. It's obvious the congregation will have to endure this sermon to its bitter conclusion. But now suddenly a new sound is added to the frantic squawking of the two desperate doves and the tired burbling of the champagne fountain. From down below come the shouts of some unforgiving paddleball players. "What's the *&%$!ing deal with these *&%$# birds?" Bride and groom each grab and bird and toss it without comment. The last two sacrificial birds flutter sadly down to their rendezvous with the paddleball athletes.

The congregation is left with some unintended but nevertheless important messages: Marriages are forged in the middle of maddening, often confusing circumstances. Expect the unexpected in your relationship. And, when it comes to communicating to the world and to each other, don't rely on birds. Try using words.

23. SEVEN MEDIDATIONS
(First appearing on Luther Seminary's
on-line devotional 'God-Pause')

NEHEMIAH 8 What happens when God's word is proclaimed? The story of Ezra's reading of the law describes the response of the hearers. Attentive listeners responded with 'Amens', upraised arms, bowing, weeping and finally celebrating. Those of us who've been called to preach the gospel yearn for some sign that our words are touching minds and hearts. A nod or a smile is encouraging, even a frown or a puzzled look is helpful. I have preached in Lutheran churches in the US, in Central and South America so I am used to (or resigned to) mostly respectful silence. A worshipper in one of my Brazilian Lutheran congregation once spoke up during a sermon and the entire crowd almost fell off their pews! I have also preached in a few Pentecostal and Baptist churches where "Amens" and encouraging words are part of the tradition. We all need to keep in mind though that what is important is not the response given to the preacher. The vital question is: How do the hearers respond to the living Word carried in by the preacher's paltry words? That's a question that can only be answered out in the world. That is a discipleship question!

Gracious Lord, may your Word continue to move me, change me and empower me to be your disciple in this love starved world. Amen.

PSALM 19 These words were written while on a spiritual retreat at Ring Lake Ranch Wyoming, when I heard creation glorifying God.

Before the beginning

Before the beginning is silence.

Not "dead" silence for nothing yet has lived so as to die.

Not "total" silence for nothing yet is so as to be summed up.

This is the silence of before.

The silence before the beginning.

Then--the beginning.

God speaks and the silence is splintered, cracked, shattered.

God's first creation is sound.

God speaks and out of the womb of that first word, all sound is birthed.

Let there be the ringing hum of galaxies,

let there be osprey alarming and blue jay blustering;

let there be high spirited children's voices tossed into nighttime sky,

let there be nickering, neighing, and clinking metal of bits and bridle,

let there be crunching of gravel, sharp cracking of apple,

and glorious, gulping gales of laughter.

Let there be brawling bellowing thunder roaring down valleys like barrels rolling down stairs.

And yes, let there be sighing---of pine trees, and of lovers

and of the spirit as she hovers

over all that soon will come to be.

I CORINTHIANS 12:12-31A My brother was an exemplary farmer. He tended the land, worked hard and respected the danger and power of the machinery that he worked with. But one day he was in a hurry to dump a load of wheat and get back to the field. He caught his gloved hand in the grain augur. Before he could pull it back, his little finger was mangled. Clutching his bleeding hand to his chest he drove home and his wife drove him to the hospital. The surgeons sewed the dirtied and bloodied appendage back into one piece. They flooded his body with antibiotics to stave off infection. The finger was saved! But, after a few weeks he noticed that he had no feeling and no movement in the finger. The muscles and nerves were so damaged that the finger could no longer do its part. In fact, the finger actually hindered him in his work. He went back to the hospital and had the finger amputated. Using the metaphor that Paul uses in I Corinthians 12 we could say that even though the finger was in some sense a "member" of the body, it was not a partner in the body's ministry. Is our connection to the body of Christ merely a formal membership or does the lifeblood of Christ, the crackling energy of the Spirit flow through and empower us?

O God, you have lovingly made us part of the body of Christ. Continue to work in us so that your Christ-bringing Spirit might work through us. Ame

LUKE 4:14-21 "We need a mission statement." Hospitals, corporations, and congregations spend hours and hours crafting cogent and concise sentences that express their purpose. I've been involved in more than a few of those writing sessions. We have always emerged with fine statements. We have not always managed to live out the mission they so eloquently expressed. Jesus doesn't bother to craft a new mission statement for himself. He draws on Isaiah who centuries earlier articulated God's good news for those living in exile in Babylon. I am struck by how down to earth this mission statement is. The poor, the captives, the blind and the oppressed are specifically mentioned. They are the 'target audience' of Jesus' mission.

If you belong to a Christian congregation, does it have a mission statement? How does it compare to the one Jesus gives us here? Recent surveys of young people who have distanced themselves from the Christian church report that they are dissatisfied with the inward looking character of most congregations. Might these young people be the prophetic voice that we need to heed? Might they be the ones who can summon us to draw closer to the mission of Christ in this broken world?

O Lord and Master, we have been brought into your body by baptism and commissioned to follow you. May your mission so shape and guide our actions that we can truly be your disciples. Amen

LUKE 4:14-21

> A word is dead
> When it is said,
> Some say.
> I say it just
> Begins to live
> That day.

Emily Dickinson's little poem expresses the Biblical understanding of the Word. The Word is a lively, active reality that enters the world and accomplishes its work.

When Jesus finished reading the words of the prophet Isaiah in his hometown synagogue and sat down I imagine everyone expected him to expound on the text, or say a few words about the prophet. Instead, Jesus says "Today this scripture has been fulfilled in your hearing."

Can you imagine the audacity of that claim? Jesus declares, "Today, right now, in your ears, in front of your eyes, this word has become flesh. Not in some abstract, generic, ethereal way, but in a concrete, fleshly, specific way. I am the One, I am the good news you have been waiting for."

Such audacity was too much for the hometown crowd and they tried to throw him over a cliff to shut him up. But it was too late. The word was out and about, already doing its work.

Think of the words you have spoken (both good and bad) that have shaped your relationships and your reality. Think of the Good News words we hear Sunday after Sunday. "In the name of Christ and by his authority, I declare to you the entire forgiveness of all your sins." And "the body of Christ, broken for you, the blood of Christ shed for you." Powerful, active words that accomplish God's will in our lives. Words are powerful. When you receive them, expect to be changed. When you speak them, handle with care!

Almighty God, we thank you for your life giving and life changing Word. May we use our words in ways that allow life and love flourish in our midst. Amen

Lutheran Book of Worship #290, THERE'S A WIDENESS IN GOD'S MERCY

"Daddy, do you know how much I love you? I love you thiiiiis much!" She flings her little arms out so wide that she almost falls over. How wide is God's mercy? The writer of this hymn tells us: "There's a wideness in God's mercy, Like the wideness of the sea." Have you ever thought about the gift of **wideness**? What does it mean that the gifts God gives us have "wideness?" Think of the opposite of wideness: narrowness, constriction, restriction. Wideness suggests abundance, room to move and maneuver, space to grow and thrive. That is what God's love gives us.

The writer of Psalm 19 praises God and says in vs36 *You gave me a wide place for my steps under me, and my feet did not slip.* Here God's gift of wideness means the security to move forward in life. One of the praise songs sung in the Brazilian Lutheran church has these words: *O God your love is such a beautiful vista, such a beautiful open field.* Imagine God's love for you as a broad, beautiful, wide open field where you can play, work, dream, love and serve.

O God, today let us celebrate your never-ending love for us and for all creation. May we stretch out our lives in joy, may we reach out our arms and in service. Amen.

Lutheran Book of Worship, #390 I LOVE TO TELL THE STORY

How does your life tell the story of God's love? My dad had a powerful voice. In his prime, I could hear him calling me from a mile away as his voice soared through the high plains air. One of my fondest childhood memories is standing beside my dad in church singing I Love to Tell the Story. Dad could not read music but he had a strong tenor voice and when we sang this familiar melody he could rattle the windows. He never articulated his faith in spoken words but by his singing and by his living I knew that he trusted in the story of Jesus and his love. In his late 50's dad was diagnosed with cancer. He fought the disease and then the despair and depression that came in its wake. His bold voice grew weaker and weaker. By the time of his death at sixty seven he barely spoke and never sang. But across the years and the miles, his voice still echoes for me. And whenever I sing this song I imagine him singing this theme in glory and telling the old, old story of Jesus and his love.

Lord God, today we thank you for all of those who have sung the old, old story of your love in our lives. May we be faithful and bold singers of the story that never dies. Amen.

24. ORGANIZED FORGETTING
(Pondering a week in Mexico)

"Is it true that the people will be unable to survive crossing the desert of organized forgetting?" (**Milan Kundera The Book of Laughter and Forgetting,** Page 220.)

TIJUANA, MEXICO, August, 2005

Each silent cross bears a name and an age. *Carlos Alberto Silva, 19....* *Maria Helena Cardoza, 22... Samuel Felipe Salgado, 24...* Cars and battered pickups clatter past behind us. Broken asphalt, dust and gravel crunch beneath our feet. Our voices drop and we stand uncomfortably like distant relatives at a funeral wake. Leftover landing panels from the Gulf War's Desert Storm operation have been set upright and fixed to steel posts on the border. Our garbage from one US invasion reemployed to stem another. What macabre recycling! The brown, ponderous, corrugated panels stretch for miles. From the US side, the wall presents a monochrome façade designed to help *El Norte* forget the individuals and the unique stories of the *pobrecitos* from the South.

On the Tijuana side, the wall tells a different story. The people of Tijuana have created a memorial, a place of remembering. They have hung hundreds of white crosses upon the dark panels of this ugly wall. *Jose Condado, 18... Ana Carolina Hernandez, 17...* "We will not forget, we cannot forget, we dare not forget." So many people, mostly young, have died trying to cross the border. Most of them died from dehydration or sunstroke. They got lost in the canyons that etch the hills on both sides of the border or they were dumped out in the desert by some skulking 'coyote' who took their money, then shoved them out of the van and condemned them to wander in circles until their liter bottles of water had been sucked dry.

Standing on end up against the wall is a coffin with a glass lid. Inside are a skeleton and a note in Spanish: "In memory of all those unnamed whom our government refuses to include in the death toll." Evidently organized forgetting is not limited to one side of the border, or to one political system.

TECATE, MEXICO, August, 2005

The San Juan Bosco orphanage sits at the foot of a rocky, brush covered mountain on the edge of Tecate, Mexico. Three quarters of the way up the slope is the national boundary, a line on a map that determines who and whose you are. The staff at the orphanage warned us before we started hiking not to cross the *fronteira*, lest the US border patrol stationed on top of the mountain pounce on us with their helicopters. Even we US citizens cannot enter our country anywhere we'd like.

The trail climbed through scrub trees and sage, wound between boulders and zigzagged up the steep slope. About a third of the way up the slope we clambered atop a house-sized rock and savored the flicker of breeze that feebly tried to ease the late afternoon heat. As we sat there, a group of more serious climbers came up the trail. The five men and women were no better equipped than we were, but it was obvious they were not out for an afternoon hike. Each carried several bags bulging with clothes and food. We nodded to them as they passed and then watched them as they climbed a few more hundred feet and then slipped behind some brush against a rock wall.

Sometime after midnight they'd probably slide out of their shelter, stretch stiffened joints and silently slip past the monitors on top of the peak. That at least was their hope. If they could get beyond that border, catch a ride into San Diego or Santa Ana or anywhere in Orange or LA County, then they could, at least unofficially, be forgotten by both governments. They could mow lawns, cut branches, clear tables, clean hotel rooms, or pick strawberries. They could slither into the crawl space under my house where the plumbing contractor is too fat to enter. They could buy my old van with 150,000 miles on it and, unless they got caught trying to bring their children or relatives across the border, they could stay forgotten for decades.

YORBA LINDA, CALIFORNIA, August, 2005

This Sunday I will stand once again before my congregation to preach God's Word. I cannot forget my week in Mexico. I cannot forget the people, the crosses and the borders.

At the borders of life, remembering and forgetting are matters of life and death. The Bible's book of Numbers tells us that at Kadesh-Barnea, on the verge of receiving the Promised Land, the Israelites forgot the covenant at Sinai and the rescue from Egypt. They even forgot their own cries for help and remembered only the security of life under slavery. They forgot the right things and remembered the wrong things.

I wonder what those five people nearing the edge of the border needed to remember. What did they have to forget? Forget the lifeless dirt, destroyed by centuries of overuse? Forget the dead-end villages with no jobs, money, or hope? Or were these the memories that they had to save in order to propel them out into the dangerous night? Did they need to remember family and friends who pray and cry for them and no doubt hope to receive money from them? Did they need to remember the crosses on the Tijuana wall? The ones who didn't make it? Who were they crossing the border for? It is so important to remember.

Faulty remembering and selective forgetting can prove fatal. God sent the Israelites back out into the desert wilderness for forty more years of wandering until the forgetful generation died. (Numbers 14) The Israelites meandered under the blazing sun, experienced empty-handed dependence over and over again, until they finally learned to trust God enough to enter the land. With enough trustful remembering in their past, they could at last cross the border and move trustfully into their future.

But crossing borders is always risky. Things can be radically altered at borders. Attitudes and values can take quantum leaps toward new positions. As a result, at borders we are always tempted to selectively forget and remember. That is why, at the edge of the Promise Land, Moses gathers the Israelites together for one more run through of the law. This is his farewell sermon and it is, above all things, a call to remember.

But take care and watch yourselves closely, so as neither to forget the things that your eyes have seen nor to let them slip from your mind all the days of your life; make them known to your children and your children's children. Deuteronomy 4:9

But remember the LORD your God, for it is he who gives you power to get wealth, so that he may confirm his covenant that he swore to your ancestors, as he is doing today. Deuteronomy 8:18

I wonder what those five men and women carrying plastic bags across the border were remembering and what were they forgetting? I remember the stories of my own grandparents who barely survived World War I. My grandfather's family was living in Russia. Evidently they were on the wrong side of the revolution because they ended up in Siberia. Or maybe it was less a political matter and more of an ethnic one. For whatever reason, they spent fifty years in that arctic wilderness, simply lost to those who'd escaped to the US.

When the *glasnost* of the 80's reopened Russia, we discovered that our kinfolk had kept memories alive in tiny house churches led by wrinkled grandmothers who'd memorized the songs and stories of the faith and of the family. In the US, my grandmother finally made peace with the barren plains of North Dakota but she never forgot nor stopped pining for the deep green forests of northern Germany. Eighty years ago, my family was an immigrant family, aliens in a strange land. I am daily tempted to forget that fact and to righteously insist upon **my** rights in **my** land.

Once we have crossed the border we are always tempted to forget. Joshua, Moses' successor, led the people across the Jordan River into the Promised Land. His first official, public act in the new land was to order 12 men back into the riverbed, dig out twelve stones, and bring them into camp. Can you imagine those sweaty, muddy men, parting the crowd like God had parted the Jordan minutes earlier? Can you see them flinging down their stones on the grass? Thunk---"remember the powerful God who brought us to this land! Thunk---"remember the faithful God who never forgets a promise!" Thunk---"remember our God who is generous beyond all imagining!" Thunk---"remember why this God brought us here!"

At the time, it must have all seemed overly melodramatic. How could they ever forget something so world altering? But of course they did forget. The border crossing radically shifted their world. They moved from a daily blessing of manna to stuffed storage barns. They stepped away from dependence and toward satiation. Border crossings are always dangerous and the Israelites did not negotiate the journey well. *

Not too many years after Moses' warnings, they were claiming credit for what was not theirs, accepting worldly blessings as well deserved rewards rather than undeserved gifts, and snarling at the aliens and strangers seeking refuge in **their** land. God sent prophets to counteract this organized forgetting. They rose up to denounce the religious and political coalitions that promoted this fatal memory loss. The Israelites did not deal kindly with these men who tried to unearth their suppressed national memories.

This Sunday I will stand once again before my congregation to preach God's Word. I feel like Isaiah: "Woe is me! I am a man with a faulty memory, living among a people with a faulty memory!" We are a satiated people who believe satiation is a blessing. We have done our best to forget hunger, need, or dependence. The people of this congregation are the people to whom I have been called. Good people, serious people….many of them are my friends. How can I help them remember what they'd rather forget? Do I dare begin with the story of the crosses? Maybe I'd best begin with the cross that never lets me forget my own deep need for rescue and hope. Before I speak, I need to remember!

(*This language and the notion of satiation are drawn from by **The Land,** by **Walter Brueggeman**, Fortress Press, Philadelphia, 1977.)

25. NOAH, THE DOVE AND THE LEAF
(A Biblical monologue)

You all know my story, its here in your holy book: **"at the end of 40 days Noah opened the window of the ark which he had made..."** **(Genesis 8:6)**

Can you imagine what it will be like to open this window for the first time? I think I've prepared myself for the sight. But, but...Oh my heart falls....Water, water, nothing but muddy water reflecting the weak light seeping through those heavy clouds....Here and there I can see the waves beating against naked rocks, the tips of the mountains...aii!

Destroyed! Everything destroyed. I stare out over those waters and I remember the cities, the fields, the friends....Drowned. Everything and everyone drowned.

I gaze out over those waters dirty with all of the world's filth, filth from dissolved cultures and communities and congregations.

I lift up my eyes to the edge of the world...water, nothing but water...chaotic, formless, lifeless water. Inside I feel heavy, dark, lonely and, and....afraid.

Eight people and a boatload of animals—What future will we have in the middle of all this water? In the middle of this ruined world? And look, just look at those heavy dark clouds. Could more rain be on the way?

I'm telling you, anxiety clamps like a vise on my chest. I turn back inside the ark and I reach out for the raven. A great bird, dark bird, as dark as the clouds. It stands on my arm as I open the window again. With a sweep of my arm I set it free.

Its wings beat majestically. Up and up...and then it flies and flies and flies until it's just a speck on the horizon.
Could it be that it sees something? Maybe, hopefully....But bit by bit the speck grows again, larger and larger. Soon I can see its wings slowly flapping, drooping, disheartened. Finally it returns in forlorn silence. Lands on my arm. We enter the ark and the poor raven hunkers down on its perch, head bowed in defeat.

Could it be that the waters have won? Maybe this furious God who destroyed everything is angry with us too? Maybe we'll all die and one by one we'll slip into these sad waters just like everyone and everything else.

The more I look at this wrecked world, the worse I feel. I close the window on that gloomy scene. I turn back to the shadowy gloom inside. But then...then my eye falls upon the dove. My friend, my little friend the dove. You know, through all of those long days and nights of rain, this little dove kept murmuring her quiet music.

Come! I can feel her small heart beating beneath her feathers. So I try again. I open the window, I raise my arms in prayer and release my little friend. Her white feathers cut the clouds like a lightning bolt. Up, up, up she flies, there and back, circling...

O God, my God, let her find a perch, a perch for her tiny claws, something green, a plant, any sign of life in this chaos.

O no!....Slowly, slowly she descends, circles downward, like the failing note of a mourner's weeping. She lands upon my hand.

So I close the window again, and put the dove back on her perch. But look! She doesn't slump with her head down. Maybe the exercise stimulated her...or maybe she saw something out there! Just look at her. Her feathers gleam, her eyes glisten. She seems to be saying, "I'm ready---lets try again."

But I...I am not ready. I cannot bear more disappointment this day. So I wait and I wait. For seven days I wait and always it's the same: water and clouds and water. Finally on the seventh day I dare to open the window again. My little friend, the dove chuckles and clucks. She is so eager. Her tiny heart is racing.

Fly my friend, fly with God's wind on your wing. With a flurry of feathers she ascends, a white arrow against the black clouds. She circles, once, twice then shoots across the sky flying to the west, flying and flying until I lose sight of her.

And now what? Well, I wait. One hour, two hours, three hours...One thing I've learned on this trip is patience. My neck is hurting, my eyes are tired...Look! There! Flying low above the waves...my dove! But something seems different....What can it be? Here she comes, closer, closer. Is it real? Can it be? Look here she is landing on my shoulder. What's this, a new leaf? Can you hear her cooing? "Green Noah, green!"

And I, I so weary with waiting, so full of anxiety and fear, I look at this one single leaf and my heart and my body start dancing and shouting. "Hey, family, my family, come see! Green, see the green. It's life, it's hope! Lets start packing, lets start celebrating. New life is budding. God is getting a new future ready for us. Let's rejoice. Let's get ready.

Yes, there I was—an old tired man dancing with joy on the deck of that smelly old boat, waving that tiny olive leaf.

It was quite a story and it happened a long time ago. The world was very different then but you know, I think we've got a lot in common. You all aren't so different from this old tired sailor.

Your holy book says that I found favor in God's eyes and so I was saved. Well, haven't you found favor in God's eyes too and haven't you been saved in the waters of your baptism and haven't you been made God's sons and daughters? I was saved. I had a special relationship with God. But even so I suffered. I had to see the destruction of an old world. I had to face a threatening chaotic world.

You all are saved too. In your baptism God gave you that promise. But even so, let me tell you, you will suffer. That old world—that old world inside of you and outside of you—that world has got to die. Everything that doesn't reflect God's will—that all will have to die. And let me tell you when your false pride dies, when your false security dies, when your hate dies, when an unjust order dies—that my friend, that will hurt.

You are saved, I was saved. I faced a chaotic threatening world and sometimes so do you. I was anxious about the future, I imagine sometimes so are you. But let me tell you something. When your world seems uncertain, when you are anxious, when you are apprehensive. Do what I did. Send out a dove.
Hope against hope, look for signs of life.
Hope against hope. Believe!
Have faith. You see my dear brothers and sisters, faith isn't a beautiful, isolated island of happiness.
Faith is sending out a dove when you can see nothing but water.
Faith is loving that neighbor when you only receive slams in return.
Faith is struggling to build community when it seems everyone thinks only of individuals.
Faith is working for a more just world when everyone else seems to only want to get their own.
Brothers and sisters, do what I did when my dove returned with that one tiny leaf. Celebrate and prepare. Sure, I had only one tiny leaf. But for me the whole world was already green. I looked at that leaf and I saw the new earth that God wanted to give to us.

You see, faith is not having all the guarantees and then acting.
Faith is seeing the whole world green in one tiny leaf.
Faith is seeing God's full love in the caring embrace of a friend
Faith is seeing God's complete new society in the fellowship of believers.
Faith is seeing all of God's great promises in the tiny signs of hope in your life.
Your holy book tells you about Jesus, a tiny green leaf in a dead world. Hold on to that my friends, hold on to that and then you can join me and dance and celebrate forever.

26. NAOMI AND RUTH
(A Biblical drama for two voices)

My name is Elimelech. We're in Bethlehem. In the language of my people that means "house of bread." It's the hour of sunset. This is my shack and that...is my field. Look at how the wind is carving away the dirt around the roots of the wheat. What irony---there is no bread in Bethlehem, house of bread. Look! Here come my two sons, running and laughing. Mahlon is ten. Chillion is nine. Look at them, thin and tan, so healthy. How long before they stop running and sit in the shade without energy, waiting for food, food that won't come in this house of bread? The look on my face puts a brake on their running. Slowly they come up to me. Mahlon is always the most serious one. He looks out over the field getting whipped by the wind. "Looks like its wiped out huh dad?" "Fraid so son, 'fraid so..." I reach out my arms. I can feel the warmth of their young life. I hug them and I want to cry.

Elimilech stands where many fathers have stood. Economies crumble, banks close, the rains never come, or they never stop, someone gets sick. Elimilech is seeing his dreams wilt. Nothing is working out. The beautiful future he'd planned out for his wife and sons is being ripped apart by this never-ending wind.

The promise is no good: Work hard, be good, love God and you will succeed. I did all of those things but the rains didn't come again this year. The damned wind never stops blowing and now my stomach aches because I'm hungry, I'm afraid and I'm angry. My parents gave me the name of Elimelech. That means 'God is King'. Yeah right. How cruel. Here in Bethlehem this year the power of God is up for grabs. Right now I'm afraid what every man fears the most: losing control of my destiny, failing to provide for my family.

Time to eat, everybody. Soup is ready! (*the two sit at a table and bow their heads*) **We eat our thin soup in silence. Only the sound of the mocking wind fills our little home. Words...I've got words locked up inside, words that've been taking shape for weeks. Words that answer a question that he doesn't dare ask. 'They say there's food in Moab.'**

Look at her clear face, her steady eyes. She's right, I know. She sees what I don't want to see.

When the old dream dies, you've got to leave it. You've got to bury it and go. You've got to search for a new dream, a new plan, a new life. (she leaves the table. Stands and gazes outward...) **Those purple hills...on the other side, isn't that Moab? Ahhhh...look at the moon...so delicate...**

And it would have to be Moab wouldn't it? We've got to leave our land, our people, even our God and go to a place where we'll be inferior. What's the future in that?

But there's food! There's food! What's the point of talking about future if there's no food? And besides, we're together, the kids are still healthy, and who knows...maybe the hand of God will go with us.

And so, one day we climbed those purple hills. And with time we found a bit of land, a place to call home. Mahlon and Chillion grew. Their little boy thin arms filled out. Now they have the muscles of healthy young men.

I do believe my parents were prophets when they named me: Naomi—Pleasant. Because isn't life pleasant when you have food and your family is united.

But one day Elimelech dies. Too much work, too much worry—who can ever tell? They lay Elimelech in a shallow grave, dug in that foreign soil. And Naomi cries, not just for her children and for herself, but also for all of the happiness and comfort that this kind and honest man never ever had.

Now Naomi is a widow and like all widows she mourns. And like all widows the sadness slowly passes, the wound slowly heals, but it never completely stops hurting.

Shhh. The house is quiet. My boys are sleeping. They're strong young men now....In here is pain, a need to talk, to share hopes with someone. Can it be that God really came with us to this land? Moab seems like such a lonely place...

Mom, I'd like you to meet Orpah! Mom, I'd like you to meet Ruth!

My family grows like all families grow. Mahlon and Chillion get married, to beautiful highland girls. Sure, they're Moabites, foreigners but they are so kind and good. Approve? Of course I approve. To see my sons happy, to see these couples delighting in each other, to see them growing in love? Of course I approve. God can live in Moab too. I'm sure of it!

But then, suddenly Mahlon dies. Strong husband, oldest son. Dead. He joins his father beneath the soil of Moab. The family comes together in this affliction.

Too often this world is a confusing and brutal place. Soon, too soon, Chillion dies. Affliction heaped upon affliction. Walking, thinking, living become almost impossible.

Now Naomi is where many women are. Desolate, without an anchor, without a compass. She is old and without a man in a world controlled by men. She is without any support. Her God, this faithful, solid God is nowhere to be found.

Don't call me Naomi—pleasant. Call me Mara—bitter. Because God has given me great bitterness.

Naomi, Orpah and Ruth live together in a little house. Three widows, three desolate women. It could be a dismal place, but no...they care for each other. Each one cries, each one comforts—a small circle of love.

One day Orpah and Ruth come home and find Naomi packing up her few things. "Mom, where are you going?"

I'm going back to Bethlehem. I'm going back to be buried among my own people. I have relatives back there. At least they'll see I get a decent burial. Besides.....now they say they've got food again back there.

Ruth and Orpah hurry to gather their own things. There's no sense arguing with her. She's right. Life without a clan, without a man to protect you is a risky business. But they can't bear to leave Naomi. This gentle wise woman is a mother to them and a friend. She understands. She loves.

And so they begin their journey. No fanfares, no long good-byes. They simply start walking away from Moab. For Naomi it's a painful pilgrimage. She leaves buried in the Moabite soil a husband, two sons, a lifetime of dead hopes and a cold, dead faith.

Sandals slap, slap, slap gently in the dust. Ruth and Orpah ask small questions: How big is Bethlehem? Where will we live? They walk and they talk. But for Naomi each step becomes heavier. Heavy thoughts weigh her down.

These two fine women are daughters to me. They've become family. I can't bear to leave them, yet I can't let them come with me. I love them too much. In Bethlehem they'll be foreigners, outsiders. I'll die and they'll languish in loneliness or go back to Moab old and worn out. I can't take advantage of their loyalty.

The three come to the edge of the plain. The land of Judah stretches out beneath them. Naomi looks out with tired eyes over the vast land. She can't look at them.

Ruth, Orpah...wait! You've been good to me. You were good to my sons. I hope God will be as kind to you as you've been to me. I want you to go home to your families. You're still young. You can still have a real home with a husband and children.

She turns and with tears flowing down her wrinkled cheeks she holds her last two children and kisses them goodbye. But Ruth and Orpah don't want to leave this kind mother. They've shared so much with her. Through their tears they protest. "No, Naomi, we'll go with you." Naomi—Pleasant pulls away from them and now she is Mara bitter. She pours out a lifetime of smashed hopes.

Go back, you two. What can you possibly gain coming with me? Do you think I still have sons in my womb that can marry you? Go Back! Look out for yourselves. You've no future with me. I'm done for. And even if by some miracle I found a husband and had more sons, could you afford to wait? Ruth, Orpah, can't you see reality? God's hand has been lifted up against me...against me. And because of that, you've suffered too. So now please, for the sake of my love for you. GO!

Orpah hears the truth in these words. One more kiss, "goodbye mom" and she turns back to Moab, back toward home. But Ruth still clings to Naomi. Calmer now, Naomi grabs Ruth's shoulders.

Look, Orpah is going back to her people and her gods. It's better that way. Follow her, my daughter.

What happens next is not unusual. It happens here and there in the lives of many people. No, it's not unusual. But it is important, very important. In fact it is one of the things that makes life and faith possible. What happens now is that Ruth does not leave. She does not leave Naomi. Naomi-Mara has forgotten something. Faithfulness doesn't always make sense. Naomi's arguments are all solid. Ruth knows that her future is dark, that she'll be a foreigner in Bethlehem and yes that she could easily live and die a widow. But faithfulness doesn't always do the sensible thing. The bond between Ruth and Naomi stands above all other facts, above all other realities.

She turns back and looks into her mother-in-law's weary face. "Don't ask me to leave you or to stop following you. Where you go I will go, where you live, I will live. Your people shall be my people. Your God shall be my God. Where you die I will die and there will I be buried. God destroy me if even death parts me from you."

I can say no more. I've run out of arguments. Besides, when I look into Ruth's determined eyes, I remember the faithfulness of my sons. I remember the deep faithfulness of my husband. And yes...I even remember the faithfulness of my God.

So, Naomi falls silent. She takes her daughter's arm and they continue their journey. Two women bound together by love, respect and faithfulness. There is no NEW sign that God still cares, no NEW promise that all will be well. There are only two women walking the lonely road to Bethlehem. But life and yes, even faith, seem a bit more possible because these two walk together.

27. GABRIEL'S TRUMPET
(A Biblical dialogue)

A little over 2000 years ago in the highest heavens the angel Gabriel was practicing on his trumpet. He was one of the Almighty God's top angels, reserved for extra special events. But for the past thousand years he'd been just sitting around heaven. Now, even for an angel that can be a long time. So he just kept practicing, keeping his lips and lungs in shape for the Almighty God's next big thing. Then one day…..

Gabriel! Come here I need you!

(Whoa, when the Almighty God calls you, your know it!) Yes, God, here I am. Ready and at your service. (Hey, guys, take it from me, the Almighty is excited and that is good news. Something big is a comin'!)

Gabe, you know I've had my long term 'save the world' plan. Well, I've decided on my next big move.

Great. So where's it going to be this time? China? You know they've had a long and ancient civilization—very cultured people. Or how about Egypt? Can't go wrong with them, powerful and great architects. The Greeks would be a great choice—I mean poetry, literature, philosophy—they've got it all. No? Oh yeah, of course. Rome. How could I not see it. Greatest empire of all time. Great infrastructure. And that military? What a fighting machine. So, I'm off to Rome!

Gabriel, Gabriel, come on, you've been around me for a long time. You know better than that. Remember the little joke the angels tell?

Ohhh yeah. 'God decided to choose and he chose the Jews…….' Yeah, yeah, I thought maybe we'd be –you know—moving on up a little.

Gabriel, are you not one of my top messengers? Were you not one of the first angels created? You should know by now that "moving on up" is not my style.

Sorry, Almighty God, I guess I've been listening to the world a bit too much. I'll grab my wings and my trumpet and head right on down to Jerusalem. Jerusalem is not a bad place; pretty, got a great temple…..

Nazareth

What?

Nazareth, I'm sending you to Nazareth.

Nazareth? Where on earth is Nazareth? I've never heard of it, your prophets never mentioned it. I can't even find it on my GPS.

Don't worry Gabe, I'll give you the directions. It's a little village in Galilee.

Galilee? Excuse me, Almighty God, isn't Galilee off the beaten path? I mean its full of unchurched, uncouth, rowdies. It's the boondocks, its...

Gabriel, do you think you're telling me something I don't already know?

Ahh, no, of course not, excuse me Almighty. I just....Well I guess I can't quite figure out how your big salvation move can start in a podunk town in the boondocks. I just can't figure it out.

Yes, Gabe, that's the beauty of it! Its something you simply can NOT figure out. Its not something any angel can figure out or any human can figure out. You can only accept it as a God thing or not. But you can't figure it out. It's going to be a total surprise.

OK, God, gotcha. A total surprise. I like to surprise people. A great trumpet blast usually gets people's attention reaaalll quick. So, whose the lucky guy in Nazareth? The mayor, the commander of the army?

Surprise Gabriel, its not a guy. It's a woman! Actually she's a rather youngish woman around fifteen.

You're killin' me here God. I will go, of course I'll go, I am your faithful messenger. But you're going to send me all the way to the boondocks of Galilee, to the podunk town of Nazareth, to blow the trumpet for a fifteen year old girl??

Actually Gabriel,.... about that trumpet...

What? Does it needs polish? Hey, I can get right to work....

No, Gabriel, I'm thinking that for this gig you might want to leave the trumpet home.

No trumpet? No trumpet? God, you are making the biggest salvation move in the history of the world and you don't want a trumpet? What am I missing here?

Gabriel, I know, I know, you've been waiting for centuries, and I promise you, before the whole story is over, you'll blow trumpets till your lips are numb and you'll get to shout and sing until your angel vocal chords are aching.

But right now, I need you to deliver a message that is so shocking, so audacious, ...why if we added your great trumpet blasts the girl might die of fright right on the spot. That wouldn't be good. You can understand what I'm saying, can't you?

I guess.... So, what's this audacious message you want me to deliver?

Ahhh, Gabriel, its so amazing, so awesome; If I dare say so, its my best plan ever. I have decided that the only way to save this broken world is to enter into it. The only way to save all of these little lost humans is to become one of them.

Become human? You mean you're going to disguise yourself as a human being and actually go down to earth?

No, no Gabe, you don't get it. I've decided to send the part of me that I love the most into the world and become a true human being. And, I'm going to do it the way all human beings do it...I'm going to start in the womb of a woman, in the womb of that young woman in Nazareth, her name is Mary by the way.

Almighty God, let me get this straight: you plan on getting birthed into that world down there? You are willing to risk hunger and thirst and germs for the sake of those ungrateful people? You are willing to put up with diaper rash and disease, hostility and hatred just so these wretched people can love you? God, excuse me for asking, but are you that hung up on their love, do you need their love that badly?

And what if I did Gabriel? What if I did? Would that make me less God? Love is what I am, Love is what I do, Gabriel. Those men and women and children on the earth, the ones you call wretched people, they are the fruit of my love. I created them out of love, I created them so that I could love them, I created them so that they could love me. And you're right, they have wandered, messed up, and they are so lost, so confused, so scared. But I still love them. I love them enough to become one of them. I'm going to love them back into my arms. Gabriel I'm going to love them even if it kills me.

Well, you said it God, I didn't. I'm only an angel. No way in hell, or in heaven or on earth can I understand the kind of love that you are talking about. That love has gotta be a God thing. (sigh) So, I'll put my trumpet in the case and go get my wings and head off to visit the young woman in Nazareth. What did you say her name was?

Mary, Gabriel, her name is Mary.

28. JOSEPH'S FIRST CHRISTMAS
(A fiction)

Joseph stood alongside the shed and relieved himself into the dust that had been pounded fine as talc by generations of hooves. The moonlight turned his stream into an arc of diamonds as he leaned his head in exhaustion against the rough wooden wall. Drained. He was emotionally drained. The past week's travel had challenged his endurance and his body had welcomed the rest at the end of each day's journey. But this day! And now this night! Though he had walked only a few miles and despite having eaten warm food for the first time in a week, still he slumped wearily against the wall of the shed. His fatigue was overpowering. The only thing that kept him from melting into the dust was his dogged attentiveness to the soft murmurs of the village women inside as they tended to the girl.

The girl...he still had trouble thinking of her as his betrothed, as his soon-to-be wife. Before this journey, he'd talked to her very little, always with either his or her family present. They had barely spoken at all before the families had agreed that this match was suitable. Both he and the girl--her name was Mary, he'd known that for years of course--both of them had accepted this matchmaking process and the decision. That was the way of their people. And the fact that she was ten years younger than he, that too was acceptable and customary. But that was where the customary had stopped in their relationship.

A sharp cry from inside the shed jolted Joseph out of his stupor. He instinctively reached for the door and then as quickly jerked back his hand. "No men allowed," the portly midwife had growled as she scowled and pushed him out of the shed. Waiting and watching--this was exhausting him. Waiting and watching... these were not customary for Joseph.

Five months before, Joseph had sat on the bench outside the rabbi's home, waiting for him to finish his morning prayers. His knee bounced incessantly. It slowed for a moment as he noticed that the bench was one of his own and he felt quietly proud of its smooth finish and solidness. But soon the knee began dancing again, draining off just enough energy to keep him planted on the bench.

Finally the old rabbi emerged from his house. His large head was fringed with a few straggly gray hairs. His robe hung slackly on what had once been a robust body. He had been the rabbi in the town for almost all of his adult life and he looked as though he carried decades of pains and worries on his slumping shoulders. He had known this Joseph since he was a four-year old boy playing in the street. Joseph leapt up as soon as Rabbi Matthias stepped out through the doorway, but the rabbi motioned him to sit back down and with a heavy sigh lowered himself down on the bench beside the young carpenter.

"So, Joseph ben Adam, what's this urgent matter that you spoke of yesterday after Sabbath prayers? I can't imagine anything that would drag you away from your workbench to speak to your old rabbi."

"Rabbi, I …. " His knee was still now, as he looked into the dim eyes of the rabbi. He dropped his head for a moment and then stared up fiercely at the old man, "Mary, my betrothed.. she's with child."

The old rabbi smiled. He was relieved and amused, "Ahhh…. Well, such things happen. Patience and-self control are virtues not often given to the young. You are not the first couple who…"

"No, rabbi. I did not,….we did not—"

Rabbi Matthias laid his hand on the carpenter's solid shoulder, "Joseph, my boy, no need to be so beset. By the laws of God you are already wed. As the Torah clearly says, 'Once you have lain with her….'"

"Rabbi stop!" Though Joseph's words were only a bit above a whisper, they struck with the intensity of a shout. He jerked to his feet as though stung and he stood looking down at the old man who looked up at him through rheumy eyes..

"The child is not mine, it cannot be mine. I swear by the name of my father and grandfather I haven't touched the girl."

"But, but… Whose then can it be? I know this girl, I knew her parents, even her grandparents I knew. This Mary, this young girl…she is so reticent, so modest,…so, so…timid. I can't believe she would.. Joseph are you sure?"

"Rabbi, I'm a plain man. I work with my hands. I measure and cut and shape. I understand things that I can hold on to. Rabbi, there is something here that a carpenter can't grasp."

He then told Rabbi Matthias about his encounter with Mary two days ago. Joseph had been walking slowly holding onto the hand of Andrew, his three year old nephew. They and his brother James and his wife and children were going toward their home. Mary was walking with her parents and younger sister and brother. Joseph smiled and nodded as she and her family passed. Mary usually smiled demurely and then dropped her veil over her face. But now she stared intently at him and even swung her head back gazing at him as they passed. She held it until she and her family rounded the corner.

He had never seen that look on her face. Was it fear? Longing? Desire? Anger? He was still puzzling what it meant when suddenly she was at his side, clutching his wrist as tightly as one of his wood clamps. "Come, please, I must tell you." Her hoarse whisper was urgent but not frantic or panicked. She pulled on his arm with a strength and a self confidence that stunned him.

She tugged him into the shade of a narrow alleyway, then dropped his arm, and bowed her head. His eyes slowly adjusted to the shadows as he gazed at this slim bowed figure before him. But her head was bowed only for an instant. She quickly raised her eyes to his, as though she had suddenly remembered she was no longer the modest maiden, and was now...What was she? The strong, stolid carpenter stood rooted and wordless.

She spoke, and her voice was clear and direct. "I must tell you. Something has happened. I can't expect you to understand this or even to believe me." Her gaze was so charged, he took a step back. Against all custom, all tradition, she stepped forward and seized both his hands, "I've been visited by a messenger from the Lord. He told me I was to have a child by the Spirit." Her eyes pleaded with his, and he thought maybe there was a sob hidden in her resolve. "Did you hear, not by the flesh but by the Spirit."

Joseph looked down at this girl, this girl who was to be his bride. Dusky eyes brimming with tears and fervor, cheeks flushed, full lips shiny with saliva, slender hands kneading his calloused paws. He lost most of her words in the thunder of his confusion. *"This girl is a stranger to me. She has been my neighbor for years, she has played with my sisters, she has been formally betrothed to me, yet in this moment she is as alien to me as an Egyptian princess."*

The girl released his hands and half turned toward the street. She spoke quietly, "Joseph, I know what the Torah says about your rights, about what you can do if you find me pregnant."

He ran his rough hands through his hair, shook his head and finally managed to speak, "Mary, I'm lost. I'm not even sure what you are telling me. But I do know I'd never harm you."

The girl turned back to him, bowed her head, "Thank you. If I had thought you would I'd never have come to you today." Now she took his arm again and led him out of the alley. He followed mutely, struck dumb by her boldness. "I am leaving tomorrow to visit my cousin in Ein Kareem. The messenger told me she too is pregnant." As they reached the street, she dropped his arm, and looked up at him with a smile playing across her young face, "I will travel alone. When I get back, we'll have to talk."

Joseph finished his story and sat down quietly beside the rabbi who continued to silently contemplate the ravens as they flew in and out of the date palm tree next to the synagogue.

"Well?" Joseph was trying to be patient but...he had work to do! "Well, what?" the rabbi replied.

"Well---well,.... What do you think? What does this mean? What should I do?" His burly hands were raised up as if he was speaking more to heaven than to the old man beside him.

"Three questions, son, you want me to answer three questions? What do I think? I am an old man and thinking is hard these days. What does it matter what I think? What does it mean? That is a better question. What does it mean to you, to her, to our Lord? Yes, a better question, but who can answer that now, at the beginning of the story? What should you do? That's the best question. That's the question that pulled you away from your work this morning isn't it? Yes, a good faithful son of Israel should always ask that question, 'what should I do?' So, what do you think you should do?"

"Rabbi, she is gone visiting her cousin but when she comes back, if she comes back, everyone will see and the talk will begin, like it always does." Joseph jumped to his feet and started pacing in front of the bench.

"If my family doesn't take her in, sooner or later her family will put her out. Maybe the elders won't stone her, but no one will help her. If I don't step forward, no one will."

He stopped and watched the morning mist melting in the valley. Now he spoke more to himself than the rabbi, "And what if what she says is somehow true? What does any of this have to do with me?"

The rabbi stood up slowly and it was possible to imagine that once, before the years had eroded his frame, he'd been as robust and strapping as Joseph. He put his arm around the young man.

"Young man, you're asking the right questions. That's more important than having the right answers. Go home, get back to work, keep asking the questions. When the right time comes the answers will come too."

Joseph had taken the rabbi's advice. Mary had come back some months later. A few weeks after her return, one morning he looked up from the board he was shaping and there she was, standing in the doorway, holding her belongings in a bundle upon her bulging belly. He took her home to his family. He explained nothing to them—what could he say? Surely silence was better than a story they would sneer at.

He kept at his work, Mary slipped into the routine of the household. Joseph felt things returning to normalcy, felt the gnarl of emotions in his chest begin to unwind. Then came the emperor's census decree, the demand to travel to the clan's origin, pregnancy or no pregnancy. Then came tedious travel, anxious fretting about having to deliver a baby on the road, cold desert nights, hot thirsty days. But through all of these, at least he'd been active. He'd had responsibilities, duties, things to attend to.

But this waiting! This was eroding him, this slumping in the dust outside the barn, while inside the cries grew sharper, the voices louder...this was excruciating. Then, abruptly, came a shrill, almost animal shriek that jerked him to his feet. He put his hand to the door just as he heard a tiny wail.

He pulled his hand away from the handle, let it drop at his side. What now? What did this all mean? Was he now a father? If not, then what was he? Was the Lord expecting something of him? If so, what? He stood in the moonlight, heard a whimper from within the shed and finally something within him surrendered. Control? Understanding? He unclenched his hands, stepped back and decided to wait, to wait and see if she would invite him in. To Joseph, that seemed like the right thing to do.

29. GALILEAN NIGHTS
(A conversation with Jesus)

Hey, Judas, pass me that wineskin, will ya.

Here, catch!

Whoa,..... man, its almost empty.

You're surprised? Didn't you see the Zebedee boys when we were eating bread a couple of hours ago?

Yeah, now that you mention it, those sons of thunder were really roarin'! Where are they by the way?

Those two? Can't you hear 'em? They're conked out over by those bushes.

Wine'll do that to you! How about the rest of the guys?

While you were up the hill praying, Peter convinced everybody to go into the town. Claimed he had a cousin who might be up for company.

Yeah, that's Peter's gift isn't it? Knows somebody in every town. He's just a party waiting to happen. Ahhh, to be young again!

What do you mean, young again? You're not old.

Big difference between 25 and 30, you know. After 30, I became an official responsible adult. But hey, Judas, why didn't you go with the gang?

Well, Jesus, I ...well...you know. I thought somebody should stay and ah, well...protect you.

Hah, hah. I've got the sons of thunder right there in the bushes. Their snoring alone would send a whole legion stampeding in terror!

Ha, you're right there. But seriously, Jesus, soldiers aren't the problem. It's hoodlums. Out here, people are barely feeding their children. The Romans crush them with taxes so they've got nothing, and nothing to lose. Desperate robbers and thieves....that's what these damn Romans have turned us in to.

Sure, Judas, I suppose you're right. Guess I should say thank you. But you know I didn't invite you along to be my bodyguard.

I...OK...Well, you know, Jesus, I'm not sure why you did invite me. I mean, I'm glad you did, sure, but I guess, well... I was hoping I could be more useful.

Useful...hmm. Interesting choice of words, Judas. Useful in what way?

I don't know... I thought by now we'd have some plan, some strategy that we'd be moving forward on.

How do you know we're not?

We're not <u>What?</u>

How do you know we're not moving forward on some plan?

How could we be? We haven't set any timetables, we haven't had any strategy meetings...unless I wasn't invi—, I mean OK, so maybe I wasn't invited. Sorry if I—.

Judas, hey brother! Calm down. You should know by now I'm not a secret meeting kind a guy. With me, 'What you see is what you get.'

Oh, Jesus, that's a good one! What I see is a good Jew who dresses shabby like the rest of us. I see a guy who laughs with the little ones and cries with the lost ones. All of that I see, all of that I get. But when you start talkin' with that up country twang I swear even the birds stop to listen. Then, when you start tellin' your stories—the Lord of heaven be my witness—power dances and crackles in the air. And don't even get me started about yesterday and those loaves and fishes. 'What you see is what you get.' Yeah right, brother Jesus!

OK, OK, you made your point. But Judas, what if its all in the seeing?

Whaddya mean?

Remember yesterday afternoon when we were walking north out of Capernaum and we saw that fox?

Yeaaah...

Remember how it blended in with the rocks and grass? Remember how long it took some of us to see it?

I don't think Matthew ever did see it.

Right. That fox was there for all of us to see. But none of us would have seen it if Nathanael hadn't spied it. You know why he saw it?

No.

Because he spent years and years taking care of his dad's sheep on the pastures south of Bethany. Haven't you notice? As we walk along he's always scanning the hills, letting his eyes roam over rocks and poke into shadows. He's trained himself to see what most of us would miss. Maybe I <u>am</u> a "what you see is what you get kind of guy." The problem is people haven't trained their eyes to see what's right in front of them.

Never thought of it that way before.... So you're sayin' there really is a plan and I just can't see it?

Aw Judas, you and your plan. Why is that so important to you? Why can't you just enjoy the journey? Wake up in the morning and see the swallows stitching the sky together, hear the ewes chewing out their lambs for lagging behind the flock, smell the bread a mother is baking for her family off in some village. Some mornings, Judas, I swear, I try to take in all of the bounty and beauty around me, and my soul aches from trying to embrace it all. Can't you just embrace it, just live it?

Oh, I do enjoy the journey. I mean I've never done anything like this before. Every day, wide-open, like an empty scroll and we fill it in as we choose. I mean such freedom, scary sometimes.... But, Jesus, how can I not think about a plan? You're the one who keeps saying "the Kingdom of God is coming." To me that means changes, big changes. And changes don't just happen, 'poof,' like some wizard's tricks. You need a plan. And as I see it, if God's kingdom is coming then that means the Roman's kingdom is going and that's not going to be easy, so—

Judas, whoa, slow down. You are definitely my impatient brother. And you're right I have been talking about the kingdom and sure that's gonna mean changes. Will you see them? Will anyone see them? How do we train our eyes? Come here, sit down on this rock. Now look up and tell me what you see.

Dark sky and stars. Should I be seeing something else?

No, no. That's what I see too. Stars. I wonder, how many of them there are?

Whoa, too many to count. Only God knows.

You think?

What?

You think God knows how many stars are in heaven?

Well, I... Sure, God knows everything.

How do you know that?

I must have learned it in the yeshiva. But, hey, what kind of God would our God be if he didn't know everything?

Ahh Judas! Now <u>that</u>'s a sweet question, a juicy, luscious question. We could sink our mind's teeth into that one and chew all night long. "What kind of God would our God be if he didn't know everything?" Well, what do you think? Maybe he'd be a God waiting for us to surprise him, a God waiting for us to make the next move, or a God waiting to see what we'll do with the world he's put into our hands. Ahh brother Judas, what a question! You've made my day. Thank you!

I...you're welcome, I guess. I don't know. To me its scary to think God gives us that much leeway, that much responsibility. I'm not sure I want it.

Yeah, but what if you already have it? What if that is God's plan? What if you and I are the ones who will have to shape tomorrow? What if..... Ahhh Judas, ...tomorrow, tomorrow. I think before tomorrow comes I need to get some sleep.

Yeah it's late. I suppose Peter and the rest will be back before long too.

Judas, If you wanna do guard duty, OK. You wanna sleep, that's OK too. Just remember, Judas, you are free. You have a choice! Goodnight.

Goodnight Jesus. I think I'll stay up awhile. Maybe I'll try to count the stars.

30. STRIVE FIRST
(A Thanksgiving sermon)

I come from a long line of worriers. Maybe worry is a component in our thick German-Russian blood, some little glitch in our DNA. Maybe it comes from growing up on a farm in North Dakota, where God knows you didn't have to try very hard to find something to worry about: hailstorms, floods, blizzards, droughts, tornadoes, just for starters. I'm sure history has something to do with it too. My dad grew up during the Depression and watched his mother, legs and arms scratched and bleeding, stomping down tumbleweed thistles in the hay wagon as they tried to gather enough food to keep their cattle alive. For Dad, worrying and fretting seemed to be all that stood between his family and chaos. If he let up for an instant, life would crumble.

Now my sister Judy is the designated worrier in the family. Some months ago my brother and I were discussing some complicated family situation. Finally he said, "Yeah it's quite a messy deal, but I'm not going to worry about it. Judy is already doing that and you know you can't outworry her!"

I imagine plenty of people in this world can keep up with my sister. All of us have done our share of worrying. The first thing we hear from Jesus in the Bible reading is "don't worry." The last thing we hear is "don't worry." Three more times during the reading we hear the same phrase from Jesus, "don't worry."

Do not worry about your life, what you will eat or what you will drink, or about your body, what you will wear. Is not life more than food and the body more than clothing? Matthew 6:25

Most of us have heard that little song, 'Don't worry, be happy.' The song reminds me of the hippie movement when I was in college. Now most of us German-Russian farm boys didn't jump into the hippie movement. It was just too big of a stretch for most of us. In the jargon of the time we were just too uptight! I had some friends who flowed with that notion of not worrying. They flowed out beyond 'not worrying' all the way to 'not caring'. Everything was laid back and cool, sometimes grungy, sloppy and even sickly, but "hey, relax man, stay cool." It's important to note that Jesus doesn't say "Don't care." He says, "Don't worry." Can we do the one without the other? How can we connect this word from Jesus, "Don't worry" with Thanksgiving, and giving thanks?

Maybe its all very simple: Jesus could be saying to all of us, "If you would stop and count your blessings, if you would look at how God has already taken care of you, if you would stop and give thanks, you could stop worrying. Just settle back in the loving, protective arms of the divine giver. Maybe Jesus is saying with just a hint of exasperation, "For God's sake, trust in your Heavenly Father's gracious giving."

This is good advice but I know how we are. We take care of what we can take care of. What we can't take care of, we worry about. When we reach our limits, we start to worry. We think that out there, beyond our control, it's not God that rules. Oh no! Out there chaos, chance and darkness reign. It's no wonder that Jesus sadly calls us people of little faith, little faith people. If our faith was as big as our worry, we could lift any mountain up by its roots.

Maybe Jesus is saying to all of us anxious, lonely, stressed out achievers, "Stop! Give thanks for your many blessings. Then not only will you reduce worrying but you will savor the joy and fullness of this blessed moment." I can hear that as a good word, can't you?

But there is more to this text and there are others who read it. The last verse of our reading goes like this: *So do not worry about tomorrow, for tomorrow will bring worries of its own. Today's trouble is enough for today.*

There is more to this text and there are others who read it. In southernmost Brazil lies the state of Rio Grande do Sul. Its state capitol is Porto Alegre, a city or over a million people. Across the river from Porto Alegre lies Guaiba, an industrial city whose air is permanently permeated by the smell of Riocell, the huge pulp mill. We lived in Guaiba for four years. We met many people and our work carried us into all sorts of neighborhoods. In a rickety housing project full of tiny wooden shacks we met Maria. She shared that name with half the female population of Brazil. Along with most of the Brazil's other Marias this Maria lived in poverty. Her husband had abandoned her and her three children. Maria got a job cleaning and cooking for a veterinarian who lived in town. She barely earned enough money to pay the rent on her tiny two-room house, yet she considered herself lucky. She at least had a job and she was allowed to take home the potato peelings after she prepared food for the veterinarian and his family. In the course of our conversations we asked her what she did for entertainment. She smiled and said, "Well, after I get home from work I make dinner and put the children to bed. Then I sit on my stool and watch their beautiful faces while they sleep." This is Maria's life. It is the life of so many people in this world. When the sun rises, and weary eyes open the first thought is "what must I do today to stay alive and keep my children alive?"

If every day is a struggle for survival what do you hear in Jesus' words? *So do not worry about tomorrow, for tomorrow will bring worries of its own. Today's trouble is enough for today. Matthew 6:34* If the Marias in this world were to stop and think, "You know tomorrow I will have to do this again, and the day after that, and the day after that….", you know what would happen? They would collapse under the burden of all those tomorrows.

For people like us who have a certain level of material security, Jesus' words are therapeutic, they comfort and call us to fret less and trust more. For our friend Maria, and for all the Marias in this world, Jesus' words are words about physical, human survival. "I will make it through this day if, and only if, I focus on this day and how to feed my children this evening. I do not have time, energy, or courage to think about tomorrow. I simply have to give tomorrow to God."

I am not telling this story to provoke pity or guilt. I tell it because it can help us focus on the heart of Jesus' message in these verses. Jesus doesn't say, "Stop worrying and relax," though that is what we'd like to hear. Jesus says, "Stop worrying and start striving. Stop worrying and start striving for the kingdom." The problem is not simply that we worry too much. The problem is that we are striving for the wrong things.

Maria's world is very small. All of her energy and time is focused on her three children and herself. Maria spends most of her waking hours thinking about how to accumulate things. She does it to keep her children and herself from physically starving.

Why do **we** spend so much time accumulating things? From what are we starving? Why is it that the malls are already overflowing with Christmas shoppers and automatic teller machines are overheating? Are we striving to satisfy a hunger that can never be filled?

Strive first for the kingdom of God and all these things will be given you as well. Matthew 6:33. If you think that it is up to you to give meaning and value to your own life, you will never stop striving, never stop starving, never stop worrying.

Strive first for the kingdom of God. Can you let God use you to give meaning, value and hope to Maria, your children, your neighbor, the stranger? *Strive first for the kingdom of God.*

Tomorrow when our family sits down to Thanksgiving dinner we will pray as we always do, "Come Lord Jesus be our guest, let this food to us be blessed, and on every table everywhere, let there be an ample share."

Tomorrow when you sit down to Thanksgiving dinner don't think about all of the many blessings you have. Instead, think of how few are the precious blessings that really count: a roof, a table, loved ones to hold your hand and heart....and an ample share, an ample share.

Tomorrow when you sit down to thanksgiving dinner, give thanks for those few things and give thanks for the humble self-giving God who keeps coming into our midst, keeps blessing us, and keeps setting us free to serve this hungry, hurting world.

31. WHAT SHALL WE DO WITH ONESIMUS?
(A play based on Paul's letter to Philemon, originally written in Portuguese, commissioned by Region Four of the Brazilian Lutheran Church and presented at its regional convention,)

SCENE ONE
Paul is seated, writing a letter. He finishes and puts it into an envelope.
Paul: Onesimus! Onesimus, come here. The letter is ready, now the rest is up to you.

Onesimus: Paul, Master...I...I can't!

Paul: "master"? You know we all have only one master, one Lord. But why can't you deliver this? I'm under house arrest but you're not. You can leave. You're free.

Onesimus: Free? If I'm free why are you sending me back to my "Owner"? If Jesus Christ is my master, how can Philemon be my owner? If I'm free then I won't go back, I won't, I—(starts to walk off stage)

Paul: Calm down, Onesimus, Calm down. Look at me. How long have you been with me?

Onesimus: I guess almost six months.

Paul: Be honest with me, son. How has our time been together?

Onesimus: Paul, its been...well...sometimes I feel like a different person. When I showed up here, I was mostly worried about staying alive, self protection. Couldn't see any way out, anywhere. Then I remembered YOU. My owner....I mean Philemon always talked about Paul, Paul this and Paul that....about how Paul was such a kind and powerful man.

Paul: (laughing) Bet you never thought you'd find me under arrest!

Onesimus: No, that was a shocker. But by the time I showed up here I was just about done for. Man, I was living in fear of the soldiers, day and night. Afraid somebody would recognize me as a run away slave. Digging through garbage, begging for money. No goals and no future except to make it through another day. I was about as low as I could get. Let me tell you, when I found you here, it seemed like an oasis in the desert. Like a true refuge. You accepted me, you didn't condemn me, you let me be useful. Yeah this place is my refuge.

Paul: Son, Onesimus....that's exactly why you have go back.

Onesimus: Wha....??

Paul: you're talking about 'refuge'. But this house isn't your refuge. I'm not your refuge. I'm just an old missionary stuck in this place. The REFUGE is bigger than both of us. We're connected to Christ, we're related to him. You come here and you experience communion and community. That's Christ alive and real. He loves you, son with a love that's bigger than fear and even bigger than death. He makes you part of his body. That's our refuge.

O: I know, I know...you're the one who told me the true Story. That's why I call you my spiritual father..

P: And that's why I call you son. But its for that very reason you have to go back to Philemon.

O: But I....

P: Listen: you're now a new person. I can see it in the love you've given me, in the way you treat others. God's will is working in your life. You're not perfect but I see something more than your ego at work in you. I'm tempted to keep you here to help me out. But Onesimus, you're a follower of Christ, and Christ doesn't isolate himself in refuges. Christ walks into this world. Son, a part of your world is Philemon. You have to go back and show this new man to him. You have to face reality.

O: Reality? Paul, I'm a runaway slave. That's reality. He can legally do anything that he wants to me. He can carve his name into my forehead, punish me however he wants to. He can even kill me! Paul I AM A RUNAWAY SLAVE!

P: Onesmius! You are God's beloved child. That's above everything. God gave you dignity and value and no one can take that from you. You're free because you belong to God. Don't every forget it. But what's the point of being free if you can't go back and face that situation in Colossae? The law says you are a thief and if you don't face Philemon, your freedom will never be a reality.

O: Oh, man...I'm so afraid....

P: I know, I know. But don't forget. Philemon is follower of Christ too. I'm praying that will change your reception. Here, take the letter...take my coat for the trip and go. Godspeed! *(they embrace and Onesimus walks offstage.)* *(Paul exits for the scene change)*

SCENE TWO

Table with 8 chairs. Afia is setting the table, placing flowers and a cross. There is a knock on the door

Afia: Philemon, get the door please.

Philemon: *(offstage)* Good evening, come on in brother.

Afia: Arquippo, How good to see you! *(They kiss on cheeks)* But...alone?

Arquippo: Lydia is coming a bit later with the kids. She went to invite that new family to our gathering.

Philemon: That's great! We might need to get more chairs. Sit my friend.

(Another knock on the door. Afia goes offstage and enters with Junia. The men stand to greet her)

Philemon: Good evening Junia. Are you alone too this evening?

Junia: For now. John stopped by to see a neighbor who is sick. But look. *(She hold out an envelope)* Something strange happened to me, just now. Someone stopped me at the plaza and said, "Are you going to Philemon's house?" I said, "Yes, why do you ask?" But he just gave me this envelope and disappeared. I didn't see who it was. It was nearly dark and he had this big cape with a hood....

Afia: That is strange. Can I see it? It only has your name on it dear. "Philemon of Colossos."

Philemon: Well then, let me open it. Hey, everyone, its from Paul! A letter from Paul!

Afia: Let's sit down. Let's hear what our brother has to say.

Philemon: *(reading)* **"I, Paul, prisoner of Christ Jesus, and Timothy, write to you, Philemon, our dear friend and coworker, and to the church that meets in your house."** Did you hear that? The letter is for all of us, it's for the congregation! Oh, listen to this: **"and to Afia our sister and Archippus our fellow soldier."**

Archippus: We sure did have some scary battles. I'll never forget that furious crowd that wanted to stone us. I still don't know how we managed to escape!

Philemon: **"Grace to you and peace from God our Father and the Lord Jesus Christ."** So, Paul is in prison again. No doubt for preaching the gospel. And here we sit in comfort....Sometimes I get to thinking....

Afia: While you think, let me read the letter. **"I always thank my God as I remember you in my prayers, because I hear about your love for all his holy people and your faith in the Lord Jesus. I pray that your partnership with us in the faith may be effective in deepening your understanding of every good thing we share for the sake of Christ."** And we have shared so many good things haven't we? This love, our fellowship, the certainty of being loved and accepted by God.

Junia: Let me read a little. Okay? **"Your love has given me great joy and encouragement, because you, brother, have refreshed the hearts of the Lord's people."** Could it be that even there in prison Paul has gotten the news of everything you've done to build up our congregation?

Philemon: Could be. Paul has lots of contacts. But I still don't know why Paul is writing to us. Read a little more.

Junia: **"Therefore, although in Christ I could be bold and order you to do what you ought to do--"**

Philemon: Aha. Now we're getting to it!

Junia: **"yet I prefer to appeal to you on the basis of love. It is as none other than Paul—an old man and now also a prisoner of Christ Jesus—that I appeal to you"**

Afia: What can it be that Paul wants?

Philemon: *(Standing up)* It doesn't matter! Whatever he is asking I will do! Paul brought me to faith, to life. He is my spiritual father. If he is asking something of me, I am ready. Let me see the letter. **"I appeal to you for my.."** *(He slowly sits and continues to read in silence)* Oh no...no... not that...

All: What? What is it?

Philemon: Its about Onesimus

Afia: Onesimus??!!

Junia: Who is Onesimus?

Afia: He is a thief, a shameless, disgraceful rat, he's a—

Philemon: OK, dear, calm down. Don't get so....so agitated.

Afia: And why shouldn't I be agitated? How much money did that guy cost us? Not to mention chaos!

Archippus: This Onesimus...Isn't he that slave of yours? The one you bought in Laodicea?

Afia: We bought him all right. And paid a pretty penny too.

Philemon: Yes, Onesimus was our slave. But about seven months ago he disappeared.

Afia: Escaped! He grabbed my gold ring and a silver necklace that my mother left me and he took off.

Archippus: Didn't you try to find him?

Philemon: Of course. We reported it to the police. We even made up some signs, offering a reward to whoever brought him back. But nothing came of it.

Junia: And now Paul has found this Onesimus. Is he sending him back to you?

Philemon: Well...it looks like it.

Afia: What luck! When that shameless jerk shows up, then we'll see who is the owner and who is the slave.

Philemon: Its not going to be that simple.

Afia: Why not? Isn't he the slave and aren't we his owners?

Philemon: Yeah...no... that is to say... Here, listen to the letter: **"I appeal to you for my son Onesimus, who became my son while I was in chains. Formerly he was useless to you, but now he has become useful both to you and to me."**

Afia: Useless? That's for sure. He was always looking for a way to escape.

Junia: But now it looks like this guy Onesimus is a follower of Christ. Isn't this what Paul is saying?

Philemon: Yeah. Exactly. Onesimus is now a follow of Jesus Christ, just like us.

Archippus: Hold on there Philemon. 'Just like us'? No way. We're not thieves or slaves.

Philemon: Well...We all were slaves, before we met Christ. Slaves of fear, of false gods...

Archippus: I know, I know. But I'm speaking of the material world.

Philemon: And don't we follow Christ in the material world?

Archippus: Well, I—

Afia: Philemon, what is it that you're thinking?

Philemon: *(quietly, handing the letter to Junia)* Read what Paul has to say.

Junia: "I am sending him—who is my very heart—back to you. I would have liked to keep him with me so that he could take your place in helping me while I am in chains for the gospel. But I did not want to do anything without your consent, so that any favor you do would not seem forced but would be voluntary."

Afia: Keep him? With our consent? No way! He is our property. We bought him legally. Now we have the right to have our property back. And we have the right to punish him too. Hey, the law must be respected. Isn't that what you're always saying, dear?

Philemon: Read on, read on.

Junia: "Perhaps the reason he was separated from you for a little while was that you might have him back forever— no longer as a slave, but better than a slave, as a dear brother. He is very dear to me but even dearer to you, both as a fellow man and as a brother in the Lord."

Archippus: How can Paul say that Onesimus is no longer a slave?

Philemon: Don't you all understand? Didn't I just say that Paul was my spiritual father? Now he writes that he is the spiritual father of Onesimus too. We are brothers, Onesimus and I. How can I be the owner of my brother?

Afia: Philemon, what are you saying?

Philemon: Afia dear, didn't you just talk about our rights?

Afia: I did.

Philemon: OK then. The law says I can do whatever I want with my slave, right?

All: Yes, sure.

Philemon: I can give him a whipping, I can break his bones, I could even kill him. The law says I can do that. But the law also says I can take Onesimus to the Forum, pay the government for his value and register him as a free man.

Archippus: No! Philemon, no! Stop. You dare not do that. You shouldn't even think of doing that.

Philemon: And why not?

Archippus: Think it through, my friend. Set free a runaway slave? Imagine the impact that would have on the other slaves. Imagine how that would affect the other owners, our friends? What would our city be like without slaves? Colossos depends on the labor of these people. Set free a slave just because he is a follower of Christ? You're thinking of something that messes with all of our lives, with the whole society. Be careful Philemon! Think about your responsibility as a community leader.

Philemon: I am thinking—

Afia: You are thinking about spending **more** money on that crook. Philemon you're going crazy. He stole precious things from our home—or are you forgetting that? I bet you Paul has no clue about that little detail.

Junia: Oh, Afia, I think he knows. Listen. **"So if you consider me a partner, welcome him as you would welcome me. If he has done you any wrong or owes you anything, charge it to me. I, Paul, am writing this with my own hand. I will pay it back—not to mention that you owe me your very self. I do wish, brother, that I may have some benefit from you in the Lord; refresh my heart in Christ."**

Afia: That Paul, asking such favors of us!

Philemon: Yeah, but doesn't he have the right? He brought us the Gospel, the good news of pardon and God's love. He opened his heart to a runaway slave. Who among us thought of doing that when Onesimus was here? And now on top of that, Paul offers to pay Onesimus' debts. Doesn't he have the right to ask this favor?

Afia: OK, OK. Maybe he has the right. But I think this is an injustice. Onesimus is the one who should pay, not Paul. Its Onesimus that has a debt with us.

Junia: But didn't Christ pay **our** debts? We were the debtors, but Christ paid for us.

Philemon: Junia! Junia! Finally someone understands me.

Afia: Philemon, I understand you. I understand too well. You think we should accept Onesimus as a member of our congregation, as our spiritual brother. I understand. But you aren't begin realistic. Create a congregation together with people like him---everyone in the same pot?

Philemon: No, everyone in the same body!

Afia: But...How can I say to him, "the peace of the Lord be with you" when what I really want to do is give him a whipping?

Archippus: Let me repeat myself Philemon. Your thinking is dangerous. It could create anarchy here, turn the entire city against us, threaten all of us followers of Christ. And another thing: Are you ready to pay a salary to your "brother" so that he can live a decent life? And the other slaves? Will you set them free too? Will you pay them too? Think this through. Think it through very carefully.

Philemon: Yeah, Archippus, you have a point. And Afia, my dear, you have a point too. And Paul also has a point. So then. What will we do with Onesimus?

(Knock on the door)

Junia: I'll get it. Its probably John, or maybe Lydia.

(she returns with Onesimus)
Afia: Onesimus!

Archippus: Onesimus!

Philemon: So now, what will we do with Onesimus?

(the scene freezes while an offstage narrator speaks)

Narrator: Centuries ago, Philemon and the Christian congregation in Collosae had to deal with Onesimus. How do you deal with the Onesimus' in your world? How are you finishing this story? What will you do with Onesimus?

32. TWO PRAYERS, TWO STORIES AND THE GOOD NEWS
(A sermon)

When I was a little boy out in New Leipzig, North Dakota my parents taught me a prayer that went like this: "Abba, liebe Vater. Amen" It's German, or at least part of it is. 'Liebe Vater' means dear father. Years later I found out that 'Abba' is an Aramaic word. 'Abba' is an intimate word, a friendly word. When a little Aramaic boy crawled into his father's lap, he said, "Abba" and it means Daddy. 'Abba' is the world Jesus used when he spoke to his heavenly Father. It is the word the first Christians used when they spoke to their God. When I said "Abba" as a boy I did not know what I was saying. But those first Christians did. They knew they could say "Abba" because in Christ God had come incredibly, lovingly close to them. They prayed "Abba" because they could taste God's love in the bread and the wine, they knew God's love in the care and compassion of their fellow Christians. The love which came from their 'Abba' was so powerful that it broke the chains of class, culture and race which enslaved people. God was their Abba and it set them free.

I knew a woman whose God was an abba God. No, she didn't call God "Abba". She wasn't Aramaic. She was Brazilian and when she prayed to God she spoke Portuguese. She said "Pai". But no matter what words she used, God was her abba. I can't say that I heard her pray, though I know she did. But when I looked at her life and at what she was doing I sensed that her God was close, loving and powerful.

Her name was Francisca. She lived in a tiny wooden shack with her five children and a sometimes there husband. Their shack, like hundreds of others in this shantytown, wallowed in the swamp near a creek—a place no one wanted, a place for poor people with no where else to go. Francisca had a beautiful smile, long black hair and a dream. "We need a day care center here," she said. "We need lots of things. What else is new?" said the other mothers. "We need a day care center here," Francisca said. "Who do you think you are? You're just as poor as the rest of us," said her neighbors.

But Francisca knew who she was. She was the beloved daughter of her Abba God. She was Somebody, so she said, "We need a day care center and we can put it in that old brick house along the creek." The city health department came and looked at the house. "Its too close to the creek and there is not enough room. We won't give you a license." They left and the curious crowd that had gathered went home. But Francisca, set free by her Abba, smiled and said, "We'll see."

In the next few weeks she visited area churches, sat in the offices of supermarket managers. She scrounged plates and cups, pots and pans, toys and games. A few people began to see what Francisca was seeing. One day they swept out the little brick house, hung up some curtains, and picked up the garbage in the yard. One day they carried in their gathered treasures, put soup on to cook and invited in the children. A day care center was born! Francisca tossed her long, black hair. "If the city wants to close us down now, they'll have to take care of these kids and start their own day care center."

Because of Francisca's dream-now-reality, the mothers in the shantytown could go out and find work, they could walk the long miles to the grocery store and carry back a few groceries. They helped when they could with food for the day care center. It never was enough and Francisca asked the churches for donations, she went from store to store. She even talked to the city government and asked for their support. Somehow she still found time to peel the potatoes, sweep the floor and wash out diapers for other people's babies. I visited her once at lunch time. There were nearly twenty children in the house and yard— hungry, ragged children. But when they came in and gathered around the table, stomachs growling and mouths watering, they waited. Francisca had taught them well. First they prayed and thanked God for their food. I wonder if they ever thanked God for Francisca. I know I did. She showed me what a disciple is. She showed me how knowing the powerful, loving Abba God can liberate you for others.

"Abba, liebe Vater. Amen" That was the first prayer and the first story. The second prayer is part of a prayer you all know well. I don't know about you but at our house before we eat we pray. The prayer usually sounds like this:

"ComeLordJesusbeourguestandletthisfoodtousbeblestAmenPassthemeat" Sounds like one long word doesn't it? The first Christians had a one word prayer too but it was much shorter. It went like this: "Maranatha!" It meant, "O Lord, come!" When they prayed it they weren't just hustling through to get to the food. When they prayed it, they meant it. "Maranatha! O Lord, come! Please come, for we have tasted your love and your peace and we cannot conform ourselves to the violence and the injustice of this age." "Maranatha! O Lord, come for we suffer along with your creatures, along with your entire creation."

"Maranatha! Your kingdom come here and now, your will be done on earth as it is done in heaven." How often have we prayed that, yet how seldom have we meant it?

Have you ever prayed "Maranatha! O Lord come!"? I did. On that day two years ago when they told me Francisca was dead I whispered, "O Lord, come!" Her sometimes around husband, a drug addict and alcoholic, had threatened her for years. She had tried to have him hospitalized, had talked to the police, had even left home for a time. But everyone was too busy with his/her own concerns to worry about one angry man. One frightfully early morning he took a pick ax to Francisca's smile, then dragged her body to the outhouse and set it one fire.

Maranatha! O Lord come, come now, come here. Let no more babies die of hunger, no more women be raped, no more young people be sent off to war, let no more Franciscas be killed.

Why is it that we Christians no longer say "Abba"? Why is it that we Christians no longer say "Maranatha"? We say "Hosanna", "Hallelujah" and "Amen". All Bible words. Why don't we say "Abba"? Why don't we say "Maranatha"? Maybe we have moved far away and our God has become a stranger with whom we dare not get to familiar, whom we dare not call "abba". Maybe we dare not say "maranatha" because we really don't want the kingdom to come. You know it only took the Christian church a few hundred years to change its prayer. Instead of saying "O Lord come!" it prayed, "Let the end be delayed." You see they wanted to show the Roman Empire that they really were nice, law-abiding people. What about you and me? Do we really want God's kingdom to come here and now? Are we ready for the changes in our lives that God's kingdom would bring, not just fine tuning to our social, economic machine, not just a few dollars more or less on our tax bill, but the kind of changes that would bring God's peace and justice to those billions of people who live right now on the edges of life? In a world of limited resources some would have to give so that others could live. Do we even dare say "Maranatha! O Lord come," when we know the Lord's coming would turn our lives upside down?

Two prayers, two stories but what about the good news? Is there any here? Yes there is, though like most really good news it also has a way of turning your life upside down. The good news is this: As Luther says in his Small Catechism, "The Kingdom of God comes of itself, without our prayer." Whether we are ready or not, whether we pray "Maranatha" or not, God's kingdom is coming and will come and will transform this world and will change your life. The good news is also this: Even though you may not be able to call your God "Abba", God is nonetheless closer to you than your very own heartbeat. When the kingdom comes into our lives and world, whether like an earthquake or a gentle invitation, the loving powerful presence of our God will sustain us. Perhaps we cannot yet pray "Abba". Perhaps we cannot yet find the courage to pray, "Maranatha!" But let us remember Francisca, and all victims of this world's violence, and remembering, let us pray that the Holy Spirit may transform our deep sighs into "Abba, Maranatha!"

33. SINGING PRAISE AT MIDNIGHT
(Thinking about worship)

It is almost midnight. Paul and Silas have every reason to ask: could there be a worse day than today? They had been seized by the local businessmen, dragged into police headquarters, accused of disorderly conduct, abused by the authorities, attacked by a mob, whipped by the soldiers and finally thrown into the darkest corner of the local hell-hole prison. Their blood and sweat mixed with the dust in their cell. The dark air is heavy with groans. This horrible day is nearly at an end. Then Paul and Silas begin to—SING! And theirs is not lament but a song of praise!

"Praise the Lord! Praise the Lord O my soul!"

Vila Colmeia is a collection of over six hundred tiny wooden houses located a few miles away from our church building in Guaiba, in southern Brazil. We have begun an outreach effort there. We hold our women's gatherings out on the street. The houses are too small and too weak for meetings. We gather amidst noise, scavenging dogs, children crying and playing. The women sit on the benches, cutting vegetables for the community soup, or trying to learn how to crochet. Some mothers come with pale faces. In this villa lurk many forces that suck away life: illness, exhaustion, abuse, constant worry about the next meal. We sit out in the street with the hot wind whispering between the little houses and we—SING. We sing praises to our God.

At worship services and celebrations, during long nights of oppression, in dark prisons of pain, on streets desolated by misery, Christians have, since the beginning, sung praises to God. Today we are still singing. For this reason we are sometimes accused of being ostriches with our heads buried in the sand, purposefully ignoring reality. Or, we are accused of being hooked on a tranquilizing religion that dulls our senses to the suffering that surrounds us. It is true that through the ages some Christians have used praise to God to drown out the neighbor's cries for help, and some have used praise to the Lord as a substitute for active solidarity with suffering brothers and sisters.

But this is not the praise of the Psalmist, nor of Paul and Silas, nor of the women in Colmeia, nor, I hope, of our members at worship. This praise is praise with a <u>memory.</u> This praise is not just an expression of gratitude because now things are going well. Certainly we should thank God for those moments. But the Psalmist's praise goes beyond this. It is not a cheap praise, praise without content. It is a praise that penetrates to the roots of our hope. It is a praise that wants to unearth the memory of the God who "keeps faith forever." (Psalm 146:6), a praise that raises up the memory of the God who executes justice for the opponent.

Paul and Silas sang praises to God because they believed that the god of violence and oppression was weaker than the God who raised Jesus. We sing praises to God on the dirty streets of Villa Colmeia because we believe that the gods who promote greed and divisions in our world have their days numbered. We sing praises at our worship services because we are convinced that the Resurrected Lord is at work in our world completing his Kingdom.

"Praise the Lord. Praise the Lord O my soul!" Praising the Lord is a subversive act, an act that subverts the world of dark cells and desolate streets. For with this act we denounce the authority of the forces of death that seek to dominate our world. When we sing "Praises with memory" we are declaring our loyalty to the God of abundant life, to the God of just distribution, to the God of sacrificial love. When we sing these praises we are declaring our commitment to the Kingdom of God.

So we here in Brazil, and we pray, you in the USA, will continue to sing praises to our God. We have no illusions, we do not want to ignore the suffering realities nor escape the hard struggles ahead. Let us sing praises to our God as a sign of our gratitude for all God has done in our lives, as a sign of our resistance to the false gods, and as a sign of our confidence in the final victory of our Lord Jesus Christ.

34. ANDRE THE SHEPHERD
(A sermon)

Andre didn't know he would be a shepherd in the annual Christmas program. Neither did we! We'd been in our small Brazilian mission congregation for only a few months. There had been no time to organize an elaborate pageant. But in a storage room we found angel's wings and shepherd's robes and we knew there'd be children at the Christmas Eve service. When the children entered the worship center we gave each of them a star with a number upon it. As a climax to our celebration we improvised a nativity scene.

We called out a number. A young girl stood up. "You will be our Mary!" She came up to front and while Lin put on her robe I called out the next number. "Ah, young man, you will be our Joseph!" Then I called three numbers. "Come forward! You'll be our shepherds." Two children scurried up the aisle. One of them came hesitantly. It was Andre and his eyes were big with surprise.

As we pulled their oversized robes over their heads I told them about the shepherds. "You shepherds are simple people, usually poor. The other people look down on you. You are tough, outdoor people. Now, where are those shepherd's staffs? Ah, here they are." I handed the staffs to Andre and his buddies. "Now shepherds, you hold on to these staffs. You need them to guide and guard your flock. You need them to protect your sheep from enemies. There are lions in those hills!"

I turned back to the congregation and began telling them about the angels. Then I felt a tugging on my robe, an urgent and persistent tugging. I turned around and looked down. There stood Andre, his serious eyes were dark pools of concern. I stooped down. He clutched my robe and whispered words that only a six-year old shepherd would admit. "Pastor, I'm afraid of lions."

First I smiled, then I began to worry. What would he do next? Run out and leave us with a hole in our cast? I began to murmur words of consolation. But Andre didn't wait to hear them. He hitched up his robe, took a fresh grip on his staff and then strode back up to his spot beside the altar. He'd registered his fear with me. Now he was back at his post. Tiny, serious eyed Andre—every inch a shepherd!

Andre, my slim little shepherd, you are for me a parable of the Christian life. Like you, all of us are called to a vocation. It is a surprise that comes from outside of us. This task, this call to serve is part of God's grace-full surprise: shepherd, street sweeper, bus driver, parent. But like you Andre, our surprise is even greater. Like you we are chosen to hear God's good news, we are selected to be witnesses to the evangel. So we go with you into the streets, fields and factories graced with good vocations and graced with good news to tell.

But there are lions! And yes, Andre, we are afraid of the lions, those beasts prowling in the dark night, icing our hearts, chilling our hopes and threatening to send us running away from our posts in an avalanche of fear. Here in Brazil the dark night is full of lions. A chaotic economic situation disturbs the rich and starves the poor. Massive corruption at all levels of government threatens to turn the entire population into individualistic cynics. "No one cares about anyone but himself, why should I be different?" Pollution destroys rivers, corporate greed destroys our Amazon forest, and the struggle for survival shatters families, marriage and hearts. Yes, Andre, there are lions here. And yes, we are afraid.

But, Andre, you did not run! Despite your fear you held firm. Was it the honor of being chosen that kept your feet firmly planted? Was it the wonder of the story that kept you there, holding the post despite your apprehension?

What will keep us from giving in to despair and cynicism? What shall keep us at our posts, living out our Christian callings, speaking and sharing the good news of God's love for this sad world?

Friends, let it be the honor of your calling. You, baptized into Christ, have been called by name, chosen and selected for a special task. Receive it, savor it, exercise it. Do not run from it.

Let it be the wonder of the story: God's love come to dwell among us, God's love here to suffer, rejoice and die with us. God's love in Christ here to save us. It is a marvelous story. Proclaim it. Live it. Shout it. Let the lions hear and let them tremble!

35. INCARNATION IN THE WAREHOUSE
(A Christmas surprise)

In Brazil, December is the heart of summer. Christmases are always hot. But in 1983 my Christmas was sweltering and surprising. For eighteen months I'd been working in a small farming community in southern Brazil as pastor of the local congregation. Along with my wife we'd also begun weekly gatherings in the poorest section of town, the favela. We met in a garage. Some people came to worship, some came curious to see the Americans who played guitar and talked with funny accents. The children came because they loved to sing. Dozens and dozens of giggling, smiling, exuberant kids milled around us whenever we appeared.

As the scorching heat of summer grew, the garage grew too small and stuffy. We began to consider what we could do for Christmas. We'd already hinted that we'd have small gifts to hand out to the children. We expected a crowd. One day as I walked through the favela I noticed an open field on a gentle slope in the middle of the shacks. How about an outdoor service? I remembered the candlelight services of my youth: tiny flames flickering in the darkness, everyone quietly singing "Silent Night". Yes, this field could be a perfect gathering place, a natural amphitheater for a gathering in the still, humid Brazilian night. I discovered that the owner was Carlos, a member of my congregation. When I told him of my plan he not only approved, he also offered to mow the grass to make it more comfortable for the audience.

Energy and excitement bubbled up as news of the special service spread. I received a special discount on boxes of small candles, a team of young people helped fill over a hundred paper bags with candies and fruit. Another team made a small manger for the telling of the Christmas story. As the sun set on the day of our candlelight service we filled the VW with the guitar, candles, gift bags and drove the half mile to the field. Clumps of people were already waiting for us. I enthusiastically sprang from the car and then jerked as if stung by a bee. I had been stung all right, not by a bee, but by a raindrop. I'd been so engulfed in preparations I'd never once glanced up. That raindrop fell from a lowering sky that obviously held a few million of its cousins. My beautiful plans were going to be washed down the hillside.

I stood in desolation as a fine mist clouded my glasses and my heart. The crowd began to murmur its sadness. At that moment Carlos drove up in his shiny pickup. He rolled down his window. "Pastor, I've got a warehouse at the top of the hill. You can move the service there. Got some bags of onions in there, but there's still plenty of room." What choice did I have? I didn't want to abandon all of the plans, nor disappoint the people, especially the children who were already racing around the soggy field like puppies chasing their tails.

When I pulled open the huge metal door to the warehouse the first thing that smacked me was the pungent smell of onions. The second thing to strike me was the crunch of dry onion skins under my feet. The floor was almost 3 inches deep in these brown parchments. If anyone dropped a lit candle in here we'd all be enveloped in flames. My disappointment was quickly overwhelmed by the waves of people that came flooding in to the onion warehouse. Soon they were everywhere, lining the walls, perched on all of the sacks of onions, covering every inch of the floor. The tide of people soon lapped at the edges of the raised platform where My wife with her guitar stood on my right and the rustic manger stood on my left. The pervasive smell of onions melded with the odor of damp clothes and sweaty bodies. The metal building reverberated with the buzz of voices and the steady patter of raindrops. This was not going to be a sweet Silent Night. To begin the festivities I taught the children my favorite Christmas chorus: Glo—ooooo—ooooo-oooooria. In excelsis deo. We sang until the metal walls rattled. Then I shouted for silence, the buzz diminished, and I began to tell the Christmas story. I told of Mary and Joseph, of how they traveled to Bethlehem looking for a place to stay, of how the hotels were all full, of how the baby was born and they had no place to lay him except in a ----I turned to the manger and stood with my mouth open. A woman holding her child was sitting on our manger.

The tide of people had swept her right onto the platform and she'd ended up perched on our manger, bouncing a two year old in her arms, listening to the story of the birth of little Lord Jesus no crib for a bed, who had no place to lay down his sweet head. I grinned and nodded at her and went on with the rest of the story. We sang another song over the buzz of the crowd and then closed with a prayer. I welcomed the children to line up for their gift bags and a tsunami of frenetic little bodies almost overwhelmed me. Finally we finished and sent everyone home into the rainy night.

As we clanged shut the warehouse doors I was struck by how our onion warehouse celebration was so much like the first Christmas. We'd made plans, but they had to be scrapped. Like Mary and Joseph we had to improvise. In less than ideal conditions something wonderful had happened. Then as now, into a crowded, humble place Christmas joy was born.

36. PATIENCE AND PERSISTENCE
(A sermon preached at the ordination of my nephew, Christopher Baesler)
New Leipzig, ND, January 23, 2005

I got a Christmas card from a friend who works in the synod office in Pennsylvania. She wrote into the card, "It was good to see your son's name on the seminary graduate list. You must be proud!" She was half right at least. Though you not my son, but my nephew, I am proud of you, and glad that I can be here today.

I've had some other reactions to my trip up here. When I told my congregation back in California that I was heading up to North Dakota, almost all of them said "BRRRR." As one of my California friends said, "Yes I'll admit it, we're all wimps when it comes to cold."

Then when I told them I was going to participate in the ordination of my nephew who had accepted a call to Shismareff, Alaska, 120 miles north of Nome, they started shaking in their boots. One ex North Dakotan said, "Brrrr" and then he said, "Shismareff? Why?"

Now I have served parishes in North Dakota, Brazil, Puerto Rico, and California and I can honestly say that people are no more sinner or less sinner in any of those places. People are no more or less lost in California than they are in Fargo, or Brazil, or Puerto Rico or Denmark or New Leipzig or Shismareff, Alaska.

Every place I have served has its particular temptations or illusions. It has its unique ways that sin rears its ugly head. You'll find that out when you get to know your people in that parish. We in California are often tempted to think that suffering and struggle can be avoided. Beautiful weather, booming economy, glamour and glitz. It's easy to think that suffering and struggle are really aberrations, abnormalities that will and should pass quickly.

Well, on this day let me remind you, Chris, let me remind you that suffering comes with the territory. Some of you might be thinking, well of course he's going to suffer, he and Michelle are camping out on the Arctic Circle. What can you expect but suffering? But you know that's not what I'm talking about. Suffering goes with the territory, not with the geographical territory, but with the vocational territory. I'm not saying that as some sort of masochist who got ordained here in 1976 and has been suffering ever since. "Hit me again it feels so good!" I'm simply stating a fact. Suffering is included in your job description. It's not the only thing that's there. There is satisfaction, joy, challenge, and reward. But there is also suffering. To be a pastor is to carry suffering.

But let's not take my word for it. Let's hear Paul, that old missionary tell us how it is. Here are the words he says to one of his pastor/ missionary trainees, a young man named Timothy:

In the presence of God and of Christ Jesus, who is to judge the living and the dead, and in view of his appearing and his kingdom, I solemnly urge you: ²proclaim the message; be persistent whether the time is favorable or unfavorable; convince, rebuke, and encourage, with the utmost patience in teaching. ³For the time is coming when people will not put up with sound doctrine, but having itching ears, they will accumulate for themselves teachers to suit their own desires, ⁴and will turn away from listening to the truth and wander away to myths. ⁵As for you, always be sober, endure suffering, do the work of an evangelist, carry out your ministry fully. I Timothy 4:1—5

Let me say just a word about this young man, Timothy. He came out of a faithful family. Earlier in his letter, Paul says to Timothy "I'm reminded of your sincere faith that lived first in your grandmother Lois and your mother Eunice and now, I am sure, lives in you." The word 'tradition' comes from a word that means to hand on. Chris, you ran a few relays in high school didn't you? *Traditio* means to pass on that which you received.

Today, along with everything else, we are celebrating a handing on. Now I wouldn't exactly say we are celebrating the handing on of your faith. The faith that carries and shapes you has a unique "Chris" shape, but your faith has upon it the fingerprints of your parents and your grandparents and your great grandparents. And I dare say, at least I hope I can say, your uncle and great uncle have contributed something to your faith too!

Today we are celebrating the handing on of a task, a commission in the Body of Christ. It is a commission that your Great grandfather, your great uncle, and your uncle also were given. Today let the one you follow be the model for your ministry. "Proclaim the gospel with patience and persistence." Repeat this, together all of you: "proclaim the gospel with patience and persistence." That's what I want you to remember today. "Proclaim the gospel with patience and persistence."

Patience. Imagine ME talking about patience! Paul says to Timothy:
Always be sober, endure suffering, do the work of an evangelist, carry out your ministry fully.

First directive: Be Sober! Now Chris, as my Dad, your Grandpa, used to say, "For cryin' out loud, don't stop grinning, don't stop laughing and smiling and finding the fun in life." I'm not too worried about that. But there are some who enter this calling who become so sanctimoniously serious they they have a hard time ever kicking back. They seem to believe that to be a Christian leader you have be this kind of somber figure. (One of the benefits of having pastors in your family: you know we're very real, sometimes very crazy people!)

Paul tells you to be sober. Don't go around getting physically drunk. That's pretty obvious. But Paul is more concerned about getting emotionally and spiritually drunk. Believe me, that can happen, and it has happened to more than one pastor. The word Paul uses here suggests that you should stay well balanced and self-controlled. Remember this, Chris: You are not the Messiah! I know you know that, but let me tell you as a fellow traveler on this road: the day will come when you will see the needs of those around you, you'll see the hugeness of the job. It will hit you like a tsunami and you will think that it's all up to you. After all you are the Pastor, and aren't they all looking to you and shouldn't you be doing more, saying more, helping more, saving more? The expectations of those you serve and your own sense of responsibility can throw you off balance. Then you start working and worrying as though you were their Savior, even though you know with your head it's not true. Stay sober Chris, proclaim the gospel with patience. Its not about you and your success.

Proclaim the gospel with persistence. Persistence! Now you and I have an advantage here. We've both been North Dakota farm boys. If there is anything a North Dakota farmer needs its persistence. Hailstorms, droughts, floods, prices that drop like a shot gunned goose—there are so many reasons to give up around here. But you and I and most of the people gathered here today know you just have to keep at in, in the good times and the bad, in season and out of season. You have to plant in the spring. You can't give up hope. Some people would call that plain old stubbornness. I'd rather call it persistence. Persistence is spiritually enriched stubbornness.

Today, Chris you are called to proclaim the gospel with persistence. In season, and out of season, keep proclaiming the life changing news of God's radical love. You'll do it in Shismareff Alaska and I've done it in southern Brazil. Let me tell you this: there will come those days when you'll look around your parish and it will seem like you're planting the gospel seed in bone dry soil, or in lifeless snow banks. You'll be tempted to think it's not worth the effort. And then there will come those days when you'll wonder about yourself; when you will feel as though YOU were the one who is dry and without life.

What do you do then? I have no other answer than old missionary Paul's answer: keep preaching. Sometimes you will have to preach before you can believe it again yourself. Sometimes you will see the word sprouting when you least expect it and then it will hit you: Blam! Oh yeah, I forgot. It's not about me. It's about God's Word, a Word that goes out and does its job. Proclaim the gospel with persistence.

Let me close with a legend that comes from the Middle Ages. Offero was the name of a man who wandered the world in search of novelty and adventure. He also was very strong. He decided he would use his strength to serve the greatest king in the world. So he put his strength at the service of the world's rulers, one after another. But always he found that each ruler was afraid of someone stronger than he was, so he kept searching. Finally he found that all rulers were afraid of the devil. He decided to serve the devil but discovered that even the devil was afraid of someone. This someone was called the Lord Jesus Christ. Ofero set out to look for him, but he couldn't find him.

One day he came upon a hermit living alongside a river. The hermit said he would only find this Lord if he stopped searching for himself and started serving others. So Ofero decided to use his strength to help people cross the river. He would put people on his back and carry them across the current. One day a small child showed up on the river bank and Ofero put the boy on his shoulders. As he started walking across the stream, the boy kept getting heavier and heavier. The current nearly swept Ofero away and he just barely made it to the other side. He collapsed on the bank and said, "How can it be that you are so heavy? It felt like I had the weight of the world on my shoulders." The boy said, "You have just carried the one who created the universe and carries the sins of the world." Ofero knew that he had found, or had been found, by the Lord Jesus Christ and he bowed to him. From that day on he was known as the Christ bearer, or in Greek "Christ ophero", or in English, "Christopher."

This is the legend that stands behind your name and here you go, out into the world, bearing the name and the message of Christ. But I'd like to give a twist to the old legend. You and Michelle are going out and you will carry the name and message of Christ. You will be living, breathing, Christians in your words and in your actions. But guess what: Christ will carry you more than you will carry him. And another thing: When you get to Shismareff, you will find Christ there too. In the community, in the pain and joy of the people, the Crucified Risen Lord will meet you, embrace you and strengthen you.

Chris: as you officially enter this ministry: Always be sober, endure suffering, do the work of an evangelist, carry out your ministry fully and proclaim the Gospel with patience and persistence.

37. "AND THEY SAID NOTHING TO ANYONE, FOR THEY WERE AFRAID."
(An Easter Sermon)

"And they said nothing to anyone, for they were afraid."(Mark 16:8)

Isn't that a strange way to begin an Easter sermon? "And they said nothing to anyone, for they were afraid." How many of you are afraid this morning? This is the land of the free, home of the brave. We live in beautiful communities. This is the land of gracious living. We're in a warm and bustling Christian church. The lilies are beautiful and fragrant. We on the staff have done our best to make this morning a wonderful worship experience and to chase away your fear.

"And they said nothing to anyone, for they were afraid." That's a strange way to begin an Easter sermon, but it's even a stranger way to end a story! We don't have the original edition of the book that the apostle Mark wrote. We just have copies of copies of copies. But most of the reliable copies that we do have end with this verse. Many bible scholars think that this is the last sentence that Mark wrote in his book. "And they said nothing to anyone, for they were afraid." What a strange way to end a story. Now if Mark really meant that to be the last word, he must have done it for a reason. Doesn't it make you wonder?

Does fear belong with Easter? The secular world says Easter means chocolate eggs and bunnies. The Christian church says Easter means celebration and victory and lilies and trumpets. Does Easter also mean fear? Are you supposed to leave here today not only full of pancakes from our Easter breakfast but also full of fear? What were these three women—Mary Magdalene and Mary mother of James, and Salome—what were they so afraid of? Maybe we **should** be afraid too. Did you ever wonder what ever became of those three women who were so scared out of their wits on Easter morning?

How daring are you this morning? Do we dare follow these three women for a few minutes? Dare look in upon their lives and hearts? Maybe we can learn something about them. Maybe we can learn something about ourselves. Let's follow them and see!

The streets of Jerusalem are as black and silent as death. The women meet at a crooked intersection, Magdalene, Mary and Salome—no one speaks. This leaden blackness before dawn is too heavy for words. Besides, they all know where they are going, what they plan to do. More words? What's the use? You can hear the faint slap-slapping of their sandals; you can catch the sharp tang of the burial spices they carry. Nothing else marks their passage through the streets of the sleeping city.

If you've ever been up all night and waited for the dawn you know how it is with these three women as they walk. Bit by bit the blackness gets paler. Bit by bit things seem to suck up the light and take on shape and form—a house, a fence, a tree—everything looks so gray and half real. Everything looks so ghostly.

Thoughts whisper in their minds. Thoughts of the death they saw two days earlier. Almost under her breath Mary whispers: "I wonder what we'll do with the stone." She had watched them on Friday night, grunting and rolling that huge stone in front of the tomb door. She whispers, "The stone, could WE roll it away?" Magdalene only shakes her head and shrugs. And they walk on.

The morning air begins to move. It tugs at their veils. The sun tugs at the horizon and a bird starts cheering it on. And the women, on a mission of love, on a mission toward death, wind their way through the garden. They wind around the shrubs and palms toward the rocky cliff into whose cold bowels they'd seen the men carry their limp, dead friend Jesus.

They round the last turn in the path. The stone—that brutal, cold, hard, fact of death—is rolled back from the tomb entrance. For an instant the world is paralyzed—the early morning breeze flutters the robes around three stone statues, three women rocked by the unknown. The only sound is the tha-thump, tha-thump of three hearts.

But then, at last, one of them moves. Salome and Magdalene and Mary edge closer. They breathe in little shallow gasps. Finally they stand at the entrance and peer into the darkness. Then slowly they are drawn in. By what? Love? Fear? Curiosity? They edge into the cave. What do they expect to find? A body? A bare stone slab? They surely didn't expect to find a man, wearing a white robe, a man sitting and smiling at them. A man who was—and they could all feel it, it was in the air—a man who was actually waiting for them.

"Don't be alarmed." His words echo in the empty cave. "You are looking for Jesus of Nazareth who was crucified. He has been raised. He is not here. Look there is the place they laid him. But go, tell his disciples and Peter that he is going ahead of you to Galilee; there you will see him, just as he told you." And then the man stops talking, as if he's said it all, as if he's said everything worth saying.

What do Mary, and Salome and Magdalene say? They say nothing. Their hearts are pressed too tightly into their throats. They take one step back and then they bolt. They run like rabbits after a gun is fired. They drop their spices, they pull up their robes and dash out into the pale sunlight and scream down the path. They are shaking like the morning leaves, they are crazy with fear. And so they run.

Mary, Salome, Magdalene—where are they going? What will they do? Why has this message made them so terribly afraid?

I could ask you the same questions. What emotions will Easter stir up in you? Where will YOU go with this Easter message? What will YOU do with this Easter news? Let's follow these three a bit farther. Maybe they can help us answer those questions.

Salome is running because she is afraid of chaos. You know what chaos is, don't you? Well Salome knows too and she is afraid of it. She didn't hear many of that man's words in the tomb. All she can remember is: "he is not here, see the place where they laid him." Salome had hoped that today would be the end of it. She'd hoped they could anoint the body, cry some more and then go home and start recovering, start recovering from the terrible death of her friend and start again to get on with living. That's what she'd hoped. But now this! Now everything is all jumbled up; even his death complicates things. Maybe his body was stolen, maybe those Roman soldiers are out looking for his followers, maybe, maybe….too many maybe's. All hell is breaking loose! Salome is a worrier and a control person. Salome is afraid of chaos and so she runs and runs and runs. She reaches home, bars the door, slams the shutters and prays and prays that the confusing, scary world will stay away.

Sometimes you and I are brothers and sisters of Salome. Death spooks us. Things we can't control, mysteries of any kind, these make us, (let's admit it!) they make us angry. As old Jack Webb used to say, "The facts, just give me the facts ma'am." Facts are what count. But lately we're not even sure we can grab onto the facts. No one talks straight anymore; everyone puts spin on his words. Loose cannon governments rattle around all over the world. Things seem chaotic.

Those of us who call Salome our sister, we come to the Easter service because it makes us feel good and it helps us forget the confusion of life. It helps us push down for a few minutes the fear that deep down at the roots of this world all hell is breaking loose. So, if the music is bright and clear, if the lilies are beautiful and the sermon uplifting, then we judge Easter a success and our optimism is reaffirmed. Yes, sometimes we are Salome's brothers and sisters.

One of the women, Mary mother of James, finally stops running. She gasps for air, chokes on her sobs, and slowly shuffles home. Mary sits on the bench beside her rough table and watches the sky brighten her window. She is afraid but no shutters or bars will protect her from what she fears. She is afraid of God. God has come too close.

She sits there in the morning hush, she feels the pounding of her heart, and her neck goes all prickly again. She knows, she knows, that God is in the vicinity. She knows that the all-powerful shaper of stars and galaxies is only a heartbeat away. She knows that if this God would just let go, would stop doing what God is doing, then it would all end—her heart would stop beating, the house would crumble, the whole universe would dissolve like a dream.

Mary didn't hear much of what the man said either. Mostly she just saw the white hot blaze of his robe. But as she sits trembling in her house, she knows that somehow God has gotten hold of Jesus and now all heaven is breaking loose. She is afraid because she cannot move, think or live without bumping in to God.

Sometimes you and I are Mary's brothers and sisters. We are afraid of that God who is on the loose. The idea of God messing around in our private lives is pretty scary. The idea that God cares about how we fill out our income tax, about our eating habits and our spending habits— whoa, that's too close for comfort! So we try to put God in the closet, in the religious corner of our lives. We feel a lot safer that way. That way we can come to God on our own terms, whenever **we're** ready.

Those of us who call Mary our sister, when we come to the Easter service we want it to make us tingle—a little bit. If it gives us just a little jolt of that Easter power, just a sip of that Easter mystery, well, then it is a success. Then we can go back to OUR human world charged up and still in charge. Yes, sometimes we all are Mary's brothers and sisters too.

And then there is Mary Magdalene. Magdalene doesn't go home at all. She isn't so sure she even knows where home is anymore. She stops running and watches Mary and Salome slip down the crooked streets. She wanders and wanders without looking where she is going. Her mind is a swirl of memories, feelings, and questions. She aches with fear— yes, with Salome's fear of chaos, and Mary's fear of God. But there is another fear, something else. She tries to grasp it but it's like a dream that slips away from you when you wake up.

Then all of a sudden the last nighthawk of the morning dives out of the sky and whoops and snaps her glazed eyes back from their wandering. She looks up. She is standing back at the hill, back at Golgotha, the place of the skull. Friday's crosses tilt and lean in the blue morning sky. Magdalene begins to understand her fear. Magdalene is afraid that the man's words are **true!** She is afraid that the dead Jesus is really newly alive. She is afraid that this bloody, ugly, damnable cross has actually been claimed by God. She is afraid that this Jesus really is going ahead of them just like he always did. If that white robed man's words are actually true, then this scarred, marked Jesus is going to be in her life forever—and she is afraid.

She knows there will be funerals, many funerals, even her own someday. There could be despair, disease, anxiety, tragedy and darkness. But if the words are truly true, then this Jesus will always be in the middle of it. And he will never let her damn it all to hell. He will always call her to hope against hope, always summon her to die for her friends, always invite her to love through her tears. Magdalene is afraid her life is never going to be the same. She is afraid that this crucified one will forever be offering her a cross. She is afraid the story is really true.

Sometimes, my friends, you and I are brothers and sisters of Magdalene. Maybe we **have to** be a little afraid. What has happened here is absolutely shattering to cool, reasonable, and calculating people. If we aren't dumbfounded, maybe we should be! What happened on that first Easter and what we remember today goes way beyond our simplistic optimism. Easter doesn't mean that now everything is OK, everything will come up roses. Sure Easter feels good, but Easter goes far beyond a simple tingly, goose bumpy feeling.

A crucified, powerless and forsaken man has become the wisdom and the power of God. He goes before us and he calls us to follow him. And sometimes, many times, we are like Magdalene and we are afraid.

What did Magdalene do with her fear? Did she let it paralyze her? Did it freeze her heart and tongue? Read the New Testament. Look around you this morning. Obviously somebody talked, somebody moved beyond fear. Maybe it was Magdalene. Can you see her?

She stands out there, staring at that empty cross, feeling the sun warming her back. She begins to whisper to herself: "He has risen, he has risen indeed. Jesus was afraid too. He trembled, he cried, he felt like a failure. He knew what it meant to be forsaken. He was hurt by life—and yet, he has arisen. If that is true then there is no place, no experience, or no emotion where Jesus cannot be. Christ is risen, he is risen indeed! If that is true, then God has done a marvelous thing. His love has conquered my loneliness and even my death. Maybe I should tell Peter, and James and John and all of them…"

Magdalene turns around and starts slowly down the hill. Each step comes quicker. She seems drawn forward. Her veil flies off in the breeze but the doesn't stop. Fear still gnaws at her, but now faith gnaws too—and faith has bigger teeth.

38. LIVING THE LIGHT IN THE MIDST OF DARKNESS
(A sermon)

This congregation, like every Christian congregation is called to be a partner in God's salvation project. You have been put here in this place and in this time for a reason. NOW is the time to look again at that reason. Now is the time to wake up and reengage. The Apostle Paul gives every congregation some guidance into how to reengage. Listen to what he says: *It is now the moment for you to wake from sleep. For salvation is nearer to us now than when we became believers; the night is far gone, the day is near. Let us then lay aside the works of darkness and put on the armor of light; (Romans 13:11-12)*

Paul uses the imagery of day and night, light and darkness to talk about your congregation's mission. How many of you have ever worn night vision goggles? Isn't it fascinating how putting on a pair of glasses can allow you to see what others can't see? You could say that Christians have night vision goggles. We stand in the same world as every other person on this planet. But by God's Spirit we can see realities that may be hidden to other people.

We look at what the world calls success and pleasure and we can see the hollowness and destruction in them. We look at what the world considers light and we say, NO, those things are darkness.

But these night vision goggles also help us to see the good that is hidden from others. The world looks at the cross and sees only suffering and death. We can see the power of God hidden in the cross, the love of God hidden in the sacrifice of parents for their children, the healing hand of God in the kindness and help neighbors give one another. The world sees only dark despair but these night vision goggles allow Christians to see the light of hope.

So, if you can see the light of hope where the world sees only darkness, what do you do about it? Paul says, you put on your armor! Or maybe since this is the first big Sunday of the NFL football season, I could say this: you suit up, put on your helmet and your pads and you go out and get ready for full contact, get ready for the battle. The battle is not against other people, the battle is against that unholy trinity: sin, death and the power of the devil. Even though they can't tear you away from Christ's embrace, they still sow seeds of hatred and fear, they still wound people, still cause divisions.

Being a Christian isn't just about sitting on a bench, or a pew and getting pep talks about how much God loves you. It includes that and yes, that is part of why we are here today. But being a Christian is actually more about running out into the playing field, onto the battlefield and giving 100% for God's salvation project. You live out the light in the midst of the world's darkness. You do that in your home, at your job, in your community. You do that as an individual and as a congregation.

Here is a little picture of living out the light in the midst of the darkness. The year was 1985. I was a pastor of a sprawling rural congregation in southern Brazil. I was also a young father. On one of my rare day's off I took my two sons, nine and six years old, on an overnight camping trip. We set up our tent alongside a gentle river that snaked around the hills. We cooked our hot dogs and played some games but the night came quickly in the valley. We went to bed very early. And, because we bedded down so early in the evening, and because we were cold, we woke up before dawn. We crawled out of our tent and discovered the world in a marvelous moment.

The stars still twinkled in the velvet sky. It was dark. It appeared as if night was ruling.But then suddenly, a bird in a tree alongside the river timidly chirped. After about twenty seconds, from another tree, another bird answered, very uncertainly. Then a third trilled with contagious joy, then another and another and within minutes there was a beautiful feathered choir singing just for us. It was dark, it appeared as if night was ruling, but already they were heralding the new day.

We listened with fascination to this heavenly music. We gazed up at the hillsides along the river. Here and there we could see lights winking, lights in the homes of the farmers. We could imagine the scenes: men and women rolling out of bed, fetching water from the well, sharpening the axe to cut firewood, heating up milk, making coffee—men and women preparing for work. It was dark. It appeared as if night was ruling, but already they were preparing for a new day.

My two sons and I stood there in the wet grass and shivered in the cold air. It was dark, it appeared as if night was ruling in the world but there were signs of the new day. No longer were the birds or the people looking back. They were only looking forward. Both birds and people were already living in relation to the day that was still to come.

For many people, reality seems very dark. It seems as though night still reigns in the world. Many people, maybe all of us are tempted to live and act in relation to the night. But God in Christ has entered this night and from within the night proclaims his victory. And now this God calls you. God calls you to live not looking back to the night, but looking forward to the new day that is to come.

39. LOIS THE BOWLER
(Remembering a saint)

Lois is one of the dearest sisters in the Messiah family. Lord willing she will celebrate her 100th birthday in July. Lois has been a bowler for many, many, many years. She used go to bowling tournaments all around the country and she would often win them. A couple of months ago I took Holy Communion to Lois and she told me this delightful story. She said, "You know Pastor, I bought tickets to the state and the national bowling tournaments this year, but I couldn't go. My eyesight is just so bad. A couple of weeks ago my lady friends invited me to come over to the lanes. I stood there and looked down the alley and you know I couldn't even see the pins. When I looked down, I could just barely see the arrow marks on the lane, so I lined up and tried it and wouldn't you know I got a strike. The next ball I got a nine and they told me which one was standing, and wouldn't you know I picked up the spare. Anyway, I ended up bowling a 150." 150! Dear Lois, who is approaching 100 and nearly blind, bowls better than I've ever bowled.

Why? Because Lois has spent a lifetime bowling. So, even without sight, even without great power, her body knows what to do. It has been trained by a lifetime of repeating the same motion over and over again.

Think about Lois and our faith life. How can we live a life of faith when the world becomes dark? How can we find confidence on God in those days when we are weak and cannot see God's hand? Look at Lois. A lifetime of practice keeps her on track, even when her vision fails. That holds true not just for her bowling, but for her faith life too. She keeps praying always and worshipping when she can. She reminds herself and everyone who visits her of her faith.

But that faith did not grow overnight. She has been practicing that faith for a long time, longer than she's been bowling. And it will carry her through. She reminds me of a verse from that old hymn *When darkness veils his lovely face, I rest on his unchanging grace; in every high and stormy gale, my anchor holds within the veil. On Christ the solid rock I stand; all other ground is sinking sand.*

I've been reading a book by with a great title: **A LONG OBEDIENCE IN THE SAME DIRECTION** by Eugene Peterson. When I think of Lois and her life I think of that phrase. When I think of the life of faith, I think of a long obedience in the same direction. God wants to use this congregation to produce exactly this: Men and women who, dare to trust in the Risen Lord day after day, dare to give themselves in love to their world, day by day, week by week, year by year—a long obedience in the same direction.

40. FRIENDS IN LOW PLACES
(A Reformation Sermon)

Traditionalism: the dead faith of the living.
Tradition: the living faith of the dead.

Nothing is worse than traditionalism. I've been to churches that go through the motions of worship. They cling to words and melodies for no other reason than that they are old or traditional. What they do is in no way connected with a living, breathing faith. Traditionalism is the dead faith of the living.

But tradition, real tradition, is something else. Tradition is that which gave life and hope to those faithful who have died. Today is Reformation Sunday when many Protestant churches celebrate their tradition.

A Mighty Fortress is Our God is a 'traditional' Lutheran hymn. Way back in the 1500's Martin Luther took a beer drinking song and wrote new words to the melody. It was a contemporary hymn. If we sing this song just to honor Luther, then we are guilty of traditionalism. If we sing this song and in our singing of it, we rejoice in the living faith of a Christian brother who has died and as we sing it we seek to connect ourselves to the power and depth of the Christian faith, then we are rightly celebrating that tradition.

Traditional and contemporary aren't necessarily two different things. What Martin Luther did was take what is contemporary and use it to honor God. That is the Lutheran tradition. We are traditional Lutherans when we take what is contemporary and use it to honor God. In being contemporary we recognize and respect our tradition.

So, just as Luther took a beer drinking melody and make it into a great hymn, I'd like to take a contemporary bar song, *Friends in Low Places,* and use it to lift up one of the central beliefs of our faith.

Garth Brooks sings a song about showing up at a wedding of a former girl friend. He arrives in his cowboy boots and everyone else is in tuxedos and fancy gowns. They're all afraid he's going to ruin the party, but he takes the groom's champagne glass and toasts them and then says, "I'll be OK cause I've got friends in low places."

Why does that phrase catch us? It's catchy because it takes a common saying and puts a surprising twist to it. What we usually hear and what we expect is: "I've got friends in high places."

During the eleven years that we lived in Brazil, we discovered that in that culture, you needed friends in high places. That is how you got things done. Banks in Brazil were chaotic. All of your utility bills had to be paid at the bank. Very few people had checking accounts, no one trusted their checks to the mail service, so you had to go to the bank to pay lights, water, and taxes. Lines were incredible. It sometimes took two hours to pay a bill. In my last parish in Brazil, the treasurer of the congregation was the vice president at the bank. He told me, "Ronaldo, when you come to the bank, don't stand in line, come to my desk, and I'll take care of you right away."

Friends in high places...they're great. The bureaucracy in that country was so complicated, the public services were so corrupt, that most of the time, the only way you could ever get anything done was by knowing somebody on the inside of the system. It was WHO you knew that determined whether you'd be a success or not. When the federal government sent the city money for the construction of five hundred small brick homes for homeless persons, the mayor put up five hundred wooden homes and he and all the city council all of a sudden had money for new additions to their already grand residences. In Brazil, you'd better have friends in high places or you were stuck.

Things aren't quite that bad in our society, but still, it doesn't hurt to have friends in high places. The last few presidential campaigns have raised issues of whether or not candidates got special favors in the military draft because they knew somebody who knew somebody who could get them a break. A year and a half ago, when I was coming back to ministry in the US and looking for a new parish I made a point of calling up my old college classmate who just happened to be a bishop in the national church. Friends in high places are a valuable asset.

But Garth sings about friends in low places. What value do these have? Standing there among the high and mighty he says, "I guess I was wrong, I just don't belong. I'm not big on social graces, think I'll slip on down to the oasis. Oh I've got friends in low places."

He says if you don't belong in the high places, if you get booted out of the high places, if you get knocked down, then what you need are friends in the low places. When you're feeling lowdown, when you need comfort and consolation, when you need an oasis, that's exactly what you need. You need friends in low places.

Almost five hundred years ago, a Bible teacher and a priest named Martin Luther posted a document on the door of the local church. Today he probably would have sent an e-mail to all of the folks in his address book or posted it on facebook. That document got copied and sent around and before long, Martin was in trouble.

You don't really care why he was in trouble. It will not change the way you live tomorrow. But here is something that you should care about, something that **could** change your life. Behind all of Luther's troubles, and behind the whole story of the Reformation, at the foundation of this part of the church that we call the Lutheran church is a fundamental, basic, radical question: **Where do you see God in your life and in your world?**

Here's what Luther said five centuries ago: *"Now it is not enough for anyone, and it does you no good to recognize God in his glory and majesty, unless you recognize God in the humility and shame of the cross."*

In other words, it's no good to see God in the high places if you can't see God in the low places. In fact, if you see God only in the high places, then you aren't really seeing God at all but are seeing your own wishful desires.

One of the first stories in the Bible is the story of the tower of Babel in Genesis 11. **Now the whole earth had one language and the same words. And as they migrated from the east, they came upon a plain in the land of Shinar and settled there. And they said to one another, 'Come, let us make bricks, and burn them thoroughly.' And they had brick for stone, and bitumen for mortar. Then they said, 'Come, let us build ourselves a city, and a tower with its top in the heavens, and let us make a name for ourselves; otherwise we shall be scattered abroad upon the face of the whole earth.'**

What's going on here? The people figured they would build a tower to God and make a name for themselves, consolidate their power. They figured, "Hey, the way to succeed is get friends in high places and what better friend to have on your side than God. So come on guys build higher."

The next verse just slays me! **The Lord came down to see the city and the tower which the mortals had built**. Its just like those old Bugs Bunny cartoons where Elmer Fudd is digging in the rabbit hole and Bugs comes up beside him and asks, "What's up doc?" And Elmer says, "I'm digging out the wabbit." Here in Babel are these silly human beings building a tower to storm heaven and make friends with the God of high places. And God comes **down** and stands at the bottom of the tower and looks at the whole project and shakes his head. "Crazy creatures, when will they ever learn?" So God confuses their language, scatters them over the face of the earth.

Where do you see God in your life and in your world? Where do you look for God?

In that great job offer that just seemed to open up when you needed it? In that wonderful victory over that dangerous illness? In that beautiful sunset or that glorious sunrise? In that gathering of believers overflowing with power and emotion? In that healthy, hearty child that has blessed your family? In all that is good and wonderful that has come in to your life? Do you see God in these things? Do you look for God in these things? Sure we do, we all do.

But how about in the other things? In the pink slip that laid you off? In that disease that does not surrender its grip? In that earthquake or hurricane? In a gathering of believers that seems to wander in a dry spiritual desert? In that child that has special health needs that put so much stress on the whole family? In things that have made your life tough and painful? Do you see God in these things? Do you look for God in these things? How hard that is!

Remember Luther's words: *"Now it is not enough for anyone, and it does you no good to recognize God in his glory and majesty, unless you recognize God in the humility and shame of the cross."*

Why is that so? Do you remember how the Bible describes the first temptation? The serpent says to Eve, "when you eat this fruit, your eyes will be opened and you will be like God, knowing good and evil." At the root of human sin is a desire to be like the God of High Places. We're not satisfied just being plain old human creatures. We yearn for more: more power, more control, more wisdom, more security, more happiness, more everything.

Because we are all trapped in that sin, because we are all sinners, we all tend to look **up** to see God. We all want to see the God who is glorious, the God who is majestic, God who is wonderful, the God who is a powerful Friend in the highest of high places. Is that wrong? Not necessarily. But let me tell you what can happen if that's the only God you are willing to look for. It has happened to the church more than once. It still happens today.

When you think your God is a Friend in High places then you can cut in front of those poor schmucks who don't have what you have, who don't know what you know. Oh, you can give them a little charity, you can send a check now and then, but basically you are one up on the others. If you think your God is a Friend in High places then you will do what you can to honor him with lofty, wondrous gifts. So in poor Brazil, where everything depends upon who you know in high places, you find cathedrals covered in gold in honor of the highest of the high. If your God is a Friend in High places then you will certainly steer clear of lowlifes and low places. If your God is a Friend in High places then you will have to try and impress him with how high you are too, show him that you deserve everything that he can pass along to you.

But if you were to come face to face with this God of the High Places, I guarantee, you would feel like Garth: "I guess I was wrong, I just don't belong." Or you might feel like Isaiah in the temple who sees God high and lifted up and says: **"Woe is me! I'm in big trouble. Now I can see myself for what I am. I am a big time sinner."** Chances are if the God of High Places really came blasting in to our lives we'd be like that fellow Job. He clamored to see God, had a bone to pick with God. When God finally confronted Job, Job threw himself face down in the dirt and said: **"Whoa, up to now I'd just heard of you, but now my eye sees you and now I despise myself and I repent in dust and ashes."**

This notion that God is only the God of High places is a notion that feeds our own sinful need to be more than we were meant to be and have more and more and more. It feeds our temptation to reach for something that doesn't belong to us. Luther saw that sin in the church of his time: a church caught up in grandiose thinking, in handing out favors, in setting itself up as the earthly representative of the God in High places.

Can you see that same kind of sin in our own society and in yourself? I can see it. I suffer from it. What is this tremendous investment we make in beautifying, redoing reshaping our bodies? Isn't it a way of resisting our creatureliness? What is this obsessive need to be plugged in, connected, wired in every minute of every day with email and Twitter and cell phones? Doesn't it reflect our desire to escape limits? What is this frantic scramble to fill up every space on the calendar? Doesn't it reveal our hidden desire to be everywhere at once, to be all things to all people, to be totally full, just like God?

Luther believed that the only way out was to go back. Back to the center of the story. Back to the cross. Do we dare do that today? Do we dare see God as a God in Low Places? God sees us still making all kinds of towers. God sees that we are still unwilling to accept that we are earthlings, creatures of the earth, still unwilling to admit that we are limited and vulnerable, still unwilling to admit that we finally are not in control. So what does God do? God comes down from the tower. God lays aside power and glory and majesty. God comes into our confusing world and God says "OK, if you want to love me, then love me here. If you want to be close to me, then come closer to the pain and hurt that comes from loving. If you want true life then give up the climbing and start kneeling."

Garth sings, "Well, I guess I was wrong I just don't belong" That is what God is saying to us in the cross. "You don't belong on towers poking their way to heaven. You belong here." We look at the cross and we see a God willing to go to the lowest of the low places. And it kills us. At least it kills that part of us that wants to be like God. Who wants to be like God if to be like God is to suffer and die?

Christ dies on the cross not to make us gods, but to make us new creatures, men and women who can accept their humanity, who can take care of this earth and who can let God be God. Christ dies on the cross to make us men and women who live by faith, who trust that at the end, at our personal end, at the end of history, at the end of all things God will have the final word. And it will be a good word.

Where do you see God in your life and in your world?

Our Lutheran tradition says we must begin with the humility and shame of the cross. As Garth Brooks puts it, when life knocks you down, when you realize that your roots are on this earth, that suffering and pain are part of the package, then its important to know that you've got friends in low places. Dear friends: in Christ you have THE friend of all friends in all of life's low places. May you find comfort and strength in that friendship.

41. AT HOME IN PARADOX
(My spiritual dwelling place)

I was a Lutheran before I was born! My mom was a Lutheran preacher's kid, three of her brothers were Lutheran pastors, and if women could have been pastors in the 40's, she might have been a Lutheran pastor too. My dad also came from a Lutheran family. In fact all of my relatives on both sides of the family were Lutherans. If anyone can claim to be a Lutheran *in utero* I surely can. I grew up going to Sunday School, Vacation Bible School, Confirmation Classes and Luther League. The only time I ever missed a church activity was when a blizzard struck or had a fever over 100!

So, both by nature and nurture I was a member of the Lutheran church. But I was also a member of the generation that grew up in the 1960's, when young people everywhere were questioning and challenging all institutions and traditions. At Christus Rex, the Lutheran Campus Ministry of University of North Dakota, I was blessed with mentors who encouraged questions. I persisted in the Lutheran tradition and was drawn to the powerful "Theology of the Cross" at the heart of Lutheran thinking and practice. During my ministry I've had the privilege of teaching courses on Luther's Theology of the Cross in Puerto Rico, California and Madagascar. I'm drawn to this theology because it refuses to give superficial, pat answers to life's deepest questions. Instead it insists that we must live within the poles of paradoxes, holding together two seemingly opposite truths.

One of this theology's key paradoxes is this: **In God's self revelation God is hidden.** Is this a paradox or is it pure illogical silliness? Let me share with you an experience from my life that may help you decide.

I worked for eleven years as a pastor in Brazil. The Brazilian Lutheran Church is strongly rooted in the German ethnic community. In many places they still call their pastor "Herr Pastor"! I began my work in in a small town called Morro Redondo. The congregation there was quite conservative and very traditional. One year to promote a children's vacation Bible school I did something that was definitely not traditional and certainly not within the conservative job description of "Herr Pastor". I painted my face white, put on a red nose and dressed up in complete clown regalia. I stepped out of the parsonage and walked down the main street handing out announcements. Many people said, "Look there goes a clown." Some people said, "Yes, and do you know that this clown is our pastor?" "No, I can't believe it." "Believe it because it is the truth."

I was revealed yet hidden. I was not a pastor disguised as a clown or a clown disguised as a pastor. I was a pastor clown (or a clown pastor!) The revelation was concrete, but also ambiguous. In order to fully understand it and appreciate it, you had to look beyond the obvious. You had to look with the eyes of faith.

A theology of the cross insists that the paradox between God revealed and God hidden is a necessary paradox so that there can be enough room for faith to be born.

Almost two thousand years ago, in order to save a rebellious world God did a very non-traditional thing: He emptied himself of divine power and took the form of a baby. Many people said, "Look, a baby." And some people said, "Yes, but do you know that this baby is our Savior?" "No, I can't believe that." "Believe it because it is the truth."

Then, this God, in order to conquer the power of death, did a very non-traditional, and by human logic, a reckless, non-conservative, senseless thing. God gave up all power and submitted himself to the power of death and died on the cross. And many said, "Look, a poor dead man." And some said, "Yes, but do you know that dead man is our Lord.?" "No, I can't believe that." "Believe it because it is the truth." There on the cross was not a God disguised as a crucified man or a crucified man pretending to be God. There on the cross was a Crucified God.

For me, this paradox between God revealed and God hidden is necessary because it creates the space where faith comes to life. The Crucified God continues to come to us in hidden ways—simple water, plain bread, regular wine, and human words. I consider these elements from an earthly perspective and I'm brought to my intellectual knees.

Not everyone may require this paradox to be a faithful disciple of Christ, but I need it. For as long as I have been conscious of being a "self" I've been tempted to give logical, and complete explanations. I am always driven to put things in order, to get things under control. I have spent a lifetime trying to convince others that I have "it" all together. This paradox drops me to my knees. I am humbled by God's insistence on defying human logic. I look at God's revelation hidden in this one we call Jesus and I murmur, "God, I believe, help my unbelief." That is the best I can do. By the grace of God it is enough. Within this paradox I have found my home.

24675512R00093

Made in the USA
San Bernardino, CA
03 October 2015